# Information Politics on the Web

# Information Politics on the Web

Richard Rogers

The MIT Press
Cambridge, Massachusetts
London, England

MIT Press books may be purchased at special quantity discounts for business or sales promotional use. For information, please email special_sales@mitpress.mit.edu or write to Special Sales Department, The MIT Press, 5 Cambridge Center, Cambridge, MA 02142.

This book was set in Sabon by SNP Best-set Typesetter Ltd., Hong Kong. Printed and bound in the United States of America.

Library of Congress Cataloging-in-Publication Data

Rogers, Richard, 1965–
  Information politics on the Web / Richard Rogers.
    p.  cm.
  Includes bibliographical references and index.
  ISBN 0-262-18242-4 (alk. paper)
  1. Information technology—Social aspects. 2. Information technology—Political aspects. 3. Web search engines—Political aspects. 4. Web portals—Political aspects. 5. Civil society. 6. Knowledge, Sociology of. I. Title.

HM851.R65   2005
303.48'33—dc22

                                                            2004050458

10   9   8   7   6   5   4   3   2   1

# Contents

# Preface

Some years ago I was asked by a newspaper to write a piece on climate change in the run-up to the Kyoto meeting. The research commenced, in the AltaVista years, with a Web search. Visiting climate change sites, I noticed that most were organizations, and all linked selectively as opposed to capriciously or randomly (in a colloquial sense). Understanding linking as a form of networking for a moment, researchers and I observed that some organizations appeared to link to their friends and acquaintances (social networking), some to authoritative bodies (reputational networking), some to their own kind only (self-referential networking), some to potential funders (aspirational networking), some to their targets (critical networking) and many to more than one type and other types, but hardly any linked to all types. The observations led us beyond a hyperlink classification scheme to undertaking organizational profiling, whereby an organization's "politics of association" in a network could be made legible. We characterized an organization's politics of association by reading between the links (and noticing the missing links, too). There is a famous graphic of a climate change network that shows Shell linking to Greenpeace, but Greenpeace not linking back. Both Shell and Greenpeace link to a number of governmental sites and receive no links in return. And governments only link to themselves. This graphic summed up a normal politics of association on display on the Web.

Working with designers and programmers resulted in a visual language as well as a piece of software. Inspired by science studies and citation analysis, the software crawls sites and analyzes linking patterns between organizations working on the same issue. Generally, the body of work that came out of those early years derived from observations about the normalcy of the realm once known connotatively as the virtual, and the everyday politics at work there. The software mapping practice was about capturing those politics.

In the years since *Preferred Placement*, where the politics of association is discussed, I have learned to respect certain novelties of the Web's culture, and ultimately to grant the medium a distinctiveness I believe it deserves. This may sound paradoxical, but it was only by doing Web-based research into its normalcy that allowed me to come to appreciate the novelty. In particular there are cultures, techniques, and devices that rank and recommend information in ways to be distinguished from the old (media) as well as analysis that seeks equations between old and new or describes imports from the old into the new. (Many of those remain, too.) Beyond the ones we created with the Web in the *Preferred Placement* period, there are further "Web epistemologies" on offer, some years in the making. In this book, I have made a first effort to describe them.

Crucially, there is also information on offer, the status of which is again distinctive from its place in other media. Put differently, the information is granted a different status through particular practices in operation on the Web (or practices that can be made operational). In this book, I inquire into whether we can take this information, or the means by which it is recommended to us, seriously. On both accounts, I believe we can, and the results disrupt some staid ideas about the quality of information and its origins.

Where we once sought to capture the politics on display on the Web, now we are interested in deploying them. This book is an attempt to locate and demonstrate anew the distinctiveness of the new medium, and propose a practice that builds with it. The aim is to employ the medium's adjudication cultures, capture the distinctive information on offer, and set out the results to challenge the status quo.

In the pages that follow, the Internet is neither a world apart, nor the world on the head of a pin. It is seen as a collision space between official and unofficial accounts of reality. In answering the question about what the Web is for, I take the medium as a place that can be made not only to reveal but also to enact politics. The practice I describe takes its inspiration from the idea that the Web is the best candidate to date to unsettle the official and the familiar. To do so, I present research on the distinctiveness of medium adjudication cultures as well as the information on the Web. Building on top of the cultures and wading into the information streams, I present tools that enact info-politics.

I would like to thank Infodrome (Amsterdam), the Dutch government project on the Information Society, for supporting the research behind this book. For undertaking the design and programming of the tools (and the images), thank you to Stephanie Hankey (Tactical Technology Collective, Amsterdam); Marieke van Dijk and Auke Touwslager (Anderemedia.nl, Amsterdam); David Heath and Suzi Wells (OneWorld International, London); Attila Egyedi, Romeo Macaria, George Popescu, and Alex Naparu (Recognos, Cluj-Napoca); Andrei Mogoutov (Ecole des Mines, Paris and Aguidel.com); and Luke Pendrell and Martin Aberdeen (formerly of Anti-Rom, London). For critical commentary, great appreciation is extended to Noortje Marres (University of Amsterdam), who has been working with me for many years. In addition, I would like to thank Krijn van Beek, Ira van Keulen, and Mei Li Vos (formerly of Infodrome); Rick van der Ploeg (former Netherlands State Secretary for Culture, Heritage and Media) Greg Elmer (Ryerson University); Andrés Zelman; Gerald Wagner; and the publication instigators, (anonymous) reviewers and editors, particularly Kirsten Foot (University of Washington). The work generally also has benefited greatly from funding by the Open Society Institute (Budapest/New York), and particularly conversations with Darius Cuplinskas and Jonathan Peizer. Thanks also to Vera Franz.

The matrices in chapter one benefited from commentary by Thomas Elsaesser at the Digital Ontologies PhD Seminar in Media Studies, University of Amsterdam, February 7, 2003.

Earlier versions of chapter two have been presented at the Infodrome Congress, The Hague, the Netherlands, April 11, 2001; the International Conference of the European Association for the Study of Science and Technology (EASST), York, United Kingdom, July 31–August 3, 2002; and at the Science Dynamics colloquium series, Amsterdam School of Communications Research (ASCoR), University of Amsterdam, September 27, 2002. Thanks to the collaborative filterers at the University of Vienna and the University of Amsterdam who did the work during the classes entitled Web Epistemologies: Reflections on the Internet as Knowledge Medium (Vienna, Autumn 2000; Amsterdam, Spring 2001) and Web Epistemologies 2.0: More Reflections on the Internet as

Knowledge Medium (Vienna, Spring 2002). Thank you to Professor Ulrike Felt, Regina Danek, and Astrid Mager in the Department of the Social Study of Science, University of Vienna. A version of chapter two has appeared in *Prometheus*, 21, 2, 2003, 195–212.

An earlier version of chapter three has been presented at the Third International Conference of the Association of Internet Researchers (AoIR), 3.0: Net/Work/Theory, Department of Infonomics (University of Maastricht) and the Maastricht School of Management, Netherlands, October 14–16, 2002; at the "Concepts of Politics" Workshop, hosted by the Department of Philosophy, University of Amsterdam and the Centre Socologie de l'Innovation (CSI), Ecole des Mines, at the Hotel New York, Rotterdam, September 14–15, 2003; and at the re-opening of the International School for Humanities and Social Sciences at the University of Amsterdam, September 25, 2003. In Maastricht, thanks to Jodi Dean for providing critical commentary and inspiring thoughts about techno-epistemology. In Rotterdam, appreciation goes to Bruno Latour for inquiring into how to follow the issues (with and without the actors). In Rotterdam and Amsterdam, Rob Hagendijk sharpened some argumentation about the Dutch GM food debate, and provided me with the official public debate "in a box." The maps (and complimentary work) were displayed and critiqued at the Next Five Minutes event, Amsterdam, September 11–13, 2003. Thanks, too, to Sylvie van den Meerendonk for data collection and Natalia Miklash for the interpretation of the Russian language sites.

Chapter four has benefited from collaborative research conducted at "Social Life of Issues 4: Competing Realities—The Social Lives of Issues on and off the Web," the workshop by the Govcom.org Foundation at the Center for Culture and Communication (C3), Budapest, Hungary, July 23–28, 2001, supported by the Open Society Institute. Early versions of the work were presented at the International *FirstMonday* Conference, Maastricht, November 4–6, 2001. Thanks to the Budapest workshop researchers from the University of Vienna, particularly Heidi Weinhaeupl, Christian Haslacher, and Christian Toepfner for doing the analysis of the Austrian newspapers and other work. Appreciation is expressed to Greg Callman and Steffie Verstappen for editing the Seattle and Echte Welvaart streams, respectively.

The arguments in chapter five have been presented at the colloquium organized with members of the Department of Communication Science, University of Amsterdam, January 11, 2003, just prior to the Dutch national elections. I would like to thank especially Kees Brants and Nick Jankowski for their critical commentary. For data collection and political platform editing, thanks to Steffie Verstappen and Jorie Horsthuis; thanks also to Arjan Widlak for implementing the system at the host, politiek-digitaal.nl, and to United Knowledge (Amsterdam) for all the help keeping it running. Appreciation is extended to Becky Lentz at the Ford Foundation, New York for supporting further reflection on the relationships between news and networks (a subject of the concluding chapter) as well as to the participants at the Govcom.org Workshop, News about Networks, de Balie Center for Culture and Politics, Amsterdam, November 10–14, 2003.

Richard Rogers
Amsterdam, December 2003

# 1

# Introduction: Behind the Practice of Information Politics

This book is an exposé of the politics of information devices on the Web, broadly conceived. It begins with a mundane but often overlooked fact: On the Web (as elsewhere) sources are in constant competition with each other for the privilege of providing information. They compete for inclusion as well as prominence in all manner of information spaces. They also compete to be the leading information, the source that matches the information requested or given at any particular time. The competition is particularly fierce for placement in authoritative spaces.

When analysts treat the extent to which the sources of information collected by authoritative spaces follow certain principles—say, inclusivity, fairness and scope of representation—the matter may be said to become political. Analysts often ask if there is a politics *behind* how a search engine or portal selects and indexes its information. This question pertains to *back-end politics*.

We begin by interrogating the back end with the aid of a Ralph Nader complaint to the U.S. Federal Trade Commission.[1] But the matter runs deeper than calls made to search engine companies to disclose information practices that are advertising in disguise. However important such exposure cases are, I wish to move from the sometimes arcane debate about search engine logics, information retrieval, and information design to a larger one about the future of the Web more generally as a space that maintains the collision between alternative accounts of reality.

One of the better terms employed these days to describe the elision of alternative accounts is *informational politics*. It is normally employed to describe how sophisticated Western governments stage democracy, not through classic forms of deliberation and representation, but with polls that pulse and other manipulative tactics that attempt to ensure media communication strategies are effective in forming views that will fall in line with the official account. Manuel Castells's discussion of informational politics provides one foothold. Richard Grusin's recent discussion of "pre-mediation" also proves helpful in conceptualizing perhaps the most extreme form of informational politics, where officially planned events, such as war, are "pre-screened" so viewers may become accustomed to the inevitable realities ahead.[2]

Here I take informational politics more broadly, and, initially, turn it on the Web. Whether this competition of sources results in inclusivity, fairness, and scope of representation, the initial query concerns whether authoritative spaces on the Web may be seen to be in alignment with official accounts of reality. In other words, are they also a forum for informational politics, however unwittingly? This, in keeping with the political analysts' principles of inclusivity, fairness, and scope of representation, is a crucial test for the state of the Web, on the *front-end*.

Discussions about back-end and front-end politics, and the extent to which they increasingly lend themselves to the demise of alternative accounts of reality, is how this book begins and ends. In between, the aim is to derive a set of principles and propose a practice that can survive a searching info-political critique. To do so, I begin with the political analysts' premises of the constitution of public-spiritedness and apply them to the back-ends and front-ends of Web projects. How do leading Web projects fare when confronted by inclusivity, fairness, and scope of representation?

Subsequently moving beyond the critique, I will propose a practice and build upon it with a series of concrete information instruments that enact information politics on the Web. The initial questions are how to adequately capture the alternative accounts of reality on offer, invest them with authority if so deserving, and rejuvenate the collision space in the public spirit.

In the narrative that follows, a particular Web epistemological practice is proposed. It strives to take seriously the means by which the cultures of the Web adjudicate. In the Web epistemology discussed below, the question is, who or what could be made to adjudicate? Here, one uses techniques to make Web dynamics adjudicate. In this sense the adjudicating agent (or agency) is being ascribed to Web dynamics, and the argument concerns which heuristics and techniques could be used to

capture and analyze them in a Web epistemology. The dynamics themselves are the result of collective human activities with machines—*registered* activities, the collective consequences of which may be out of sight
or incomprehensible to humans without techniques. Some of the evidence for labelling these dynamics out of sight or incomprehensible lies
in the increasing difficulty people have in manipulating the results of
leading search engines or tampering with the recommendations flowing
from leading collaborative filtering applications.[3] For example, the
refinement of Google's techniques (as opposed to AltaVista's) continues
to forestall manipulation, payola, and the like—a great achievement.
With the rise of authoritative spaces relying principally on non-
voluntaristic techniques—those that do not allow "self-reporting"—
opportunities arise for developing further means of capturing and
analyzing Web dynamics for the purpose of source adjudication.[4] The
purpose here is to develop a set of heuristics for doing so, and interrogate the value of the results in terms of the information politics performed. (Google, as an example of authoritative spaces discussed below,
does not fare as well as one may imagine.)

It is a bold proposal, for the cultures and spaces that adjudicate
(through, for example, collaborative filtering and hyperlink measures, as
well as particularly public-spirited manual editing practices) have a host
of problems of their own, as I discuss. But overall it is an experiment
worthy of pursuit if Internet analysts persist in posing the larger question of what the Web may be for. In this book consider the Web the finest
candidate there is for unsettling informational politics. Chapters two
through five—the realised political instruments for the Web—each may
be read as a demonstration of why and subsequently how this goal may
be accomplished.

## Back-end Information Politics

The recommendation by the American Federal Trade Commission that
search engine companies disclose paid link policies and "preferred placement" schemes was significant for Internet users.[5] That companies pay
to have their links included in search engines and for high rankings in
returns, and that seemingly neutral or objective engine returns may be
advertisements in disguise, turned out to be news to some 60% of

Internet users, as surveyed by Princeton University researchers and reported by the FTC in its recommendation.[6] The FTC decision, communicated in a letter to iWon.com, MSN.com, Netscape, AltaVista, Direct Hit, HotBot, and LookSmart, asked the companies to ensure that ads in search engine returns, whether preferred placements or paid inclusion schemes, are clearly and conspicuously marked in keeping with deceptive advertising statutes. This would bring an end to the consumer confusion, it was said; action on the part of search engine companies was favored by 80% of the users surveyed.

By pulling back the curtain on the origins of the information in search engine returns, the recommendation brings into focus a crucial point about information and a form of politics behind its delivery. We all are being invited to recognize an often-neglected point in what is sometimes thought to be a medium that flattens and equalizes the status of information: Multiple sources are vying for different information to be placed under the same generic heading in authoritative, aggregated listings. The maneuverings behind that competition—the competition, in the above case, for key words to be associated with particular sources—is one clear definition of information politics in practice. These are the politics behind information retrieval, or back-end information politics.

The stakes are great. Search engines are not merely technical but political matters, as political analysts Lucas Introna and Helen Nissenbaum point out. "[Search engines] provide essential access to the Web both to those with something to say and offer as well as to those wishing to hear and find. Our concern is with the evident tendency of many of the leading search engines to give prominence to popular, wealthy, and powerful sites at the expense of others."[7] Theirs is a plea for search engines, as the primary means of access to indexed information in the new medium, to provide full disclosure of the rules governing indexing, ranking, and other information-biasing mechanisms and schemes, including preferred placement and paid inclusion.

The Federal Trade Commission did not make such a sweeping recommendation to engine companies. The Commission followed the more limited arguments made by the filer of the complaint that set the case in motion. Consumer Alert, the Ralph Nader-headed group, only went so far as to point to the growing influence of the market on search engines ("ad creep" was the term used), and the confusion arising from mixing ads and editorial content in the graphical lay-out—a concern long on the agenda of search engine watchers. Consumer Alert did not wish to politicize the methods of indexing and ranking, that is, the search engine logics themselves.[8]

When search engine companies first unveiled their engines, they did not put ads in the search results. Results were displayed based on objective criteria of relevancy tallied by algorithms. During the last year, however, some search engines sacrificed editorial integrity for higher profits, and began placing ads prominently in the results, but without clear disclosure of this practice.[9]

Taking aim at the objectivity of search engine logics, Introna and Nissenbaum tally up the various reasons why a site is not indexed in the first place, or, if indexed, why it is not well-ranked. Where the absence of indexing is concerned, for example, it may not be in the path of crawler; it may be on a very large, partially-indexed site. Where ranking is concerned, it may not have received sufficient links; it may be an "orphan site" with no inlinks.[10]

But, more importantly, Introna and Nissenbaum, as well as other authors, go further than Consumer Alert's calls for disclosing the mixing of ads with editorial content.[11] They desire that engines and tools embody more generally another form of information politics, another back-end spirit. Engines should take up the "suite of values embodied in the ideology of the Web as public good," they write.[12] The authors enumerate a set of political and system design principles befitting this spirit—inclusivity, fairness, and scope of representation. They urge engine-makers to enquire into the extent to which any particular mix of the standard elements in their (ranking) logics—metatags, hyperlinks, pointer text, freshness—produces more public-spirited returns.

A short example may illuminate the authors' point—one made more or less forcefully on certain trade, public advocacy, and critical sites, from searchenginewatch.com to google-watch.org. In February 2003 researchers and I ran queries for the term *terrorism* in Google in an effort to grasp the extent to which the back-end politics of information retrieval may or may not be converging with more common understandings of informational politics. The sociologist Manuel Castells has provided the term *informational politics* to describe how governmental and party politics are performed not through classic government-citizen exchanges and deliberations but rather through the mediation of the press and

**Table 1.1**
An Overview by Searchenginewatch.com of Major Search Engine Companies' Preferred Placement and Paid Inclusion Schemes, with a Disclosure Rating, July 2002.

| Search Engine | Program | Notes | Disclosure Rating |
|---|---|---|---|
| AllTheWeb (FAST) | Paid Placement | "Sponsored Search Listings" sold by Overture "Start Here" links sold by Lycos | Pass (Qualified) |
| | Paid Inclusion | May occur in main results | Fail |
| AOL Search | Paid Placement | "Sponsored Links" are paid links from Google | Pass |
| | Paid Inclusion | May occur in main results currently provided by Inktomi | Fail |
| | Content Promo | "Recommended Sites" generally lead to AOL or partner content | Fail |
| AltaVista | Paid Placement | "Products and Services" links sold by AltaVista or Overture | Fail |
| | Paid Inclusion | Occurs in main results and directory listings | Fail |
| Ask Jeeves | Paid Placement | "You may find this featured listing helpful" sold by Ask | Fail |
| | Paid Placement | "You may find these sponsored links helpful" links from Overture | Fail |
| | Paid Placement | "You may find these options useful" paid links from others | |
| | Paid Inclusion | May occur in "Click Ask below for your answers" or "You may find my search results helpful" sections | Fail |
| Google | Paid Placement | "Sponsored Link" ads sold by Google appear at top and to right of main listings | Pass |
| | Paid Inclusion | None | n/a |
| HotBot | Paid Placement | "Sponsored Search Listings" sold by Overture | Pass |
| | Paid Inclusion | May occur in any results from Inktomi (look for Inktomi logo at bottom of page) | Fail |
| | Content Promo | In "Search Partners" and "From The Lycos Network" areas | Fail |

| | | | |
|---|---|---|---|
| Inktomi | Paid Inclusion | Paid inclusion program allows sites to be crawled more deeply in Inktomi's listings | n/a |
| Look Smart | Paid Placement | "Featured Listings" sold by LookSmart | Fail |
| | Paid Inclusion | Commercial sites pay for listing | Fail |
| Lycos | Paid Placement | "Sponsored Search Listings" sold by Overture "Start Here" links sold by Lycos | Pass (Qualified) |
| | Paid Inclusion | May occur in main results provided by FAST | Fail |
| | Content Promo | "From The Lycos Network" area | Pass |
| MSN Search | Paid Placement | "Sponsored Sites" from Overture | Pass |
| | Paid Inclusion | May occur in "Web Directory" info from LookSmart or "Web Pages" info from Inktomi. | Fail |
| | Content Promo | In "Featured Listings" area | Pass (Qualified) |
| Overture (GoTo) | Paid Placement | Listings with "Advertiser's Max Bid" note are paid | Pass |
| | Paid Inclusion | Unpaid results from Inktomi may have paid inclusion listings | Fail |
| Netscape | Paid Placement | "Sponsored Links" from Overture, in future from Google | Pass |
| | Paid Inclusion | None | n/a |
| | Content Promo | Within "Matching Results" | Pass |
| Yahoo | Paid Placement | "Sponsor Matches" sold by Overture | Pass |
| | Paid Inclusion | "Yahoo Express" provides fast review and possible inclusion in main listings. Mandatory annual fee for commercial areas. | Fail |
| | Paid Submission | Within "Inside Yahoo!" area | Pass |

*Source:* http://www.searchenginewatch.com, July 2002.

broadcasting media.[13] Other authors describe politics through mediation in epistemological terms—that which we come to know cannot be easily disentangled from that presented in the press and broadcast media.

At the other epistemological extreme are the Daily Me writers such as Nicholas Negroponte and Cass Sunstein. In very different manners both speak of how the Internet—especially the personal filtering of information before it arrives—encourages disintermediation and an end to a shared discourse and experience associated with common consumption of press and broadcast media.[14] Of interest to us here, in our small experiment, is the further point Sunstein makes in relation to *information exposure*. More readily, the point also relates to the "pluralism of viewpoints" principle written into certain national public broadcasting laws. To what extent are the politics at work in search engines and shown in search engine returns precluding exposure to a range of arguments?[15]

Our Google queries for *terrorism* furnished us in the top twenty results pages from the White House, the CIA, the FBI, the Heritage Foundation, a smattering of strategic studies groups at universities, CNN, and *Al Jazeera*, the Qatar-based news network. We do not wish to overstate the point that the preferred search engine—providing in 2002 what google-watch.org called "75% of all external referrals on most Websites"—would be epistemologically aligned with a particular version of arguments we may associate with the evening news, however much it may put paid to a disintermediation-through-search-engines argument.[16] We also do not wish to belabor points about bias, its origins, or its consequences, particularly in relation to Google's PageRank method. The political analysts of search engines already have done so.

Of greater importance here is which overall Web dynamics one should capture, and which sorts of politics may different uses of Web dynamics put on display or into action. Google, for example, looks primarily at links and the pointer text describing the link, though their logics are ever-evolving. Those sites receiving the most links with pointer text corresponding to the key word query will be privileged in the returns. Since the results may be increasingly aligning with the mediated, we are interested in asking whether the Web need be so aligned. In other words, which kinds of overarching logics and methods may be brought to bear in order to undertake another information politics—perhaps one more in tune with the political and system design principles enumerated by our analysts—inclusivity, fairness, scope of representation? (See table 1.2.)

## Front-end Information Politics

Before discussing which Web dynamics and capturing methods may be available to enact more public-spirited information politics, as well as how to build upon those principles, there are further cases to be discussed. The next case is more classically political and allows us to begin to make some further distinctions about information politics. The UK online Citizens' Portal is a different kind of authoritative space in the new medium where a form of information politics has been in play. To the initiators, the portal is a place where citizens can have their say in open discussions about issues in an ostensibly deliberative forum. Unlike the back-end maneuverings to which Ralph Nader alerted us, in what the sociologist Ulrich Beck would call the "sub-political," deal-making arena, the UK online Citizens' Portal is more formally political in the sense of hosting citizen discussions and consultations in a governmental framework.[17] It is an ideal e-democracy project, whereby citizens and their viewpoints are offered access to other citizens and to the government, outside of the realm of informational politics—that is, without the mediation of day-to-day pollsters, more formal opinion researchers, or the media.[18] In December 2001, over a year after the project properly commenced, twelve discussions were taking place on children, families,

**Table 1.2**
Web epistemology matrix classifying Web projects on the basis of relationships between the following features: self-reporting (volunteering information to be indexed) and inclusivity of actors (who may wish to be included).

| | Adjudication | |
| --- | --- | --- |
| Collection Method | Inclusive | Exclusive |
| Voluntaristic | | |
| Non-voluntaristic | | Google* |

*Ranking logics and indexing methods result in exclusion, as Introna and Nissenbaum have argued.

and retirement; countryside; crime and home affairs; culture, media, and sport; defence; devolution and local government; economy and taxation; education, training, and employment; environment, housing, and transport; European and international affairs; health and welfare; and science and technology, with some 20,000 total postings.

The subject categorizations neatly match individual ministerial responsibilities. Ostensibly, the discussions are potential inputs in ongoing political debate and decision making within government.

Which information is allowed to be displayed in this e-democracy portal? What constraints are placed on the scope of issues and range of arguments discussed? When the citizens' portal was first brought into service in 2000, the contribution level was low. Citizens contributed such inappropriate content to the discussions that the government re-launched it with a registration requirement. Registration was the threshold to make way for more serious debate. Debates have been taking place, yet some elements of medium culture (for example, pseudonyms, flaming, spamming) have been stronger than the picture of serious citizen discussion the government may have in mind.[19] In the discussion lists one repeatedly encounters this message: "This message has been removed due to violation of Code of Conduct 4, please refer to Terms and Conditions for further information." Citizens often do not perform as well as envisaged, and as required.

Organizing the discussion themes by ministerial responsibility and requiring user-citizen registration are *info-political system design* decisions. Here they are made with an eye to facilitating discussion of issues on ministerial agendas. The means by which these decisions are translated onto the Web, however, have brought into focus a clash of two digital cultures. Above, mention was made of the anonymous and pseudonymous users, flaming, spamming, and list misconduct. To that list of familiar elements of one digital culture one may add to it hyperlinking, or recommendations made on sites and lists to other pages, to other points in the debates.

Together these elements of digital culture are beginning to come into conflict with the newer digital copyright and proprietary cultures, which the UK online Citizens' Portal has adopted. The site's general terms and conditions of the debate require attention. Reference may not be made to the debate by an external hyperlink without permission, meaning one may not point to the debate on the Web. The site's hyperlink policy, from the terms and conditions, reads:

You are not entitled (nor will you assist others) to set up links from your own Web sites to ukonline.gov.uk (whether by hypertext linking, deep-linking, framing, tagging or otherwise) without our prior written consent, which consent we may at our absolute discretion, and without providing a reason, grant or withhold.[20]

From a copyright point of view, the "Crown," as site author, owns the debate space. Ownership of others' content generated on one's site is not unusual in the newer proprietary Web. Efforts to disallow hyperlinks to the discussion, especially by government, are more novel. (Attempts at forbidding deep-linking by one company to a competitor have a longer history.[21])

I would like to take up two of the crucial consequences of the Crown's information politics, particularly as they are in contrast to the political and system design principles enumerated earlier. Whilst other analysts may concentrate on the regrettable level of the discussions (evidenced by the frequent resort to code of conduct messages), as well as the missed opportunities in this showcase e-democracy debate space for the Blair government, it is important to point out the kind of political debate the space's information politics author. (See figure 1.1.)

The first consequence of the Crown's information politics is one's need to "surf government" in order to participate in debate. We have a situation whereby people are asked to follow the formats of the government's online information politics—formats that constrain what counts as a contribution. The second, related consequence is that those discussions and positions that live elsewhere (on the Web) may not join the debate by referencing it in the form of a hyperlink. In principle, the debate thus is a governmental as opposed to a social debate. With the government's adoption of particular online information policies, a question arises about the government's understanding of what constitutes debate. More normatively, one may ask, should government, using these formats, author the debate?

The lack of social-ness to the debate is a consequence of the *politics of information formatting*, a front-end form of information politics. By classifying issues along the lines of ministerial responsibility instead of gleaning or grabbing them from society—issues that may be more readily

Discussions

## Crime and home affairs

Welcome to the crime and home affairs forum. You can find relevant background information on the following government websites:

Home Office
Crime Reduction
Lord Chancellor's Department

Please register and/or sign-in at the bottom of this page. Only registered users can participate in discussions on ukonline.gov.uk.

Discussions | Top | Go to Topic | Threaded View | Search     Newer Topic | Older Topic

### Best Idea for Decades!

Author: silly
Date:  14-12-01 18:49

And a Police Chief realises that the war on drugs has failed - Time to Legalise!

What do you think?

### Re: Best Idea for Decades!

Author: truebrit
Date:  14-12-01 20:15

I think it has to be determined which is worse the effects of drugs or the effects of criminalising them.

An important aspect is that if people are damaged taking drugs at least the innocent are spared.

It may be that legalisation with a full awarenes drive maybe the way to go. When people see the drug damaged derelicts walking the streets then popular culture may turn against drug use.

**Figure 1.1**
Sample discussion from the UK online Citizens' Portal, captured on December 14, 2001.

embedded in the medium—and by disallowing external connections to the discussions and other common features of medium culture, instead of inviting them, the government excludes itself from the public-spirited Web, with inclusivity, fairness, scope of representation, and now social-ness, as its organizing principles.

One of the rationales behind the overt practice of information politics—editing the Web, editing out social debate and the rest of the medium—is illuminated in another governmental portal project in the Netherlands. Here it becomes clearer that information politics may also be viewed as reassurance projects—a means of creating sites with trust-worthy information, providing safe places to go on the Web. The Web as safe haven—now defined as an info-political system design practice (to be criticized)—was once most frequently associated with America Online. AOL has traded on the Web as danger zone, as rumor mill—a chaotic space of questionable purveyors of information.[22] The dangers of the Web, or the more radical view that the Web can harm or even kill you, arise from occasional reported cases of people obtaining pharma-ceuticals and other products (and contacts) through unregulated (Web) channels and using them improperly, as is discussed in chapter two on Viagra. There we discuss how one may take advantage of the Web's proximity to street culture and unpalatable realities, instead of denying or whitewashing them—which in itself may be dangerous. That discus-sion is prefaced with current practices for averting Web danger, as well as how they could be rethought. We do so by thinking about the extent to which the editing initiatives are benefiting from knowledge of medium culture and Web dynamics (back-ends on the Web, if you will), and whether they translate into public-spirited information provision (front-end Web).[23]

The idea of the Web as dangerous place arrived in 2001 in the Nether-lands at the Ministry of Health, and a Web site solution was put forward. It is an editorial approach that seeks, vets, and authorizes a small set of "information partners" before allowing materials of theirs to appear on the Ministry's sponsored initiative—the health kiosk portal gezondheidskiosk.nl. To gain some perspective on the strategy, it is helpful to list the defining elements of trustworthy information as listed on the gezondheidkiosk's site. Information is trustworthy if the follow-ing is known: its purpose (*doel*), target group, source, date of publica-tion, and background context (with further references provided, if possible). Information also must be non-commercial. At the time of writing, nine information partners have met these (socio-epistemological) requirements for providers of trustworthy information.[24]

If one of the greater challenges of the medium for Web epistemologists is to overcome the impression (and occasional reality) of people acting on untrustworthy information, the health kiosk's goals are comprehen-sible and the project is fundable. The goals fit with the pictures in our heads of how a group of editors might go about defining criteria for evaluating sources, assuming they are unburdened by a familiarity with the medium cultures and Web dynamics—apart from its reputation as chaotic and potentially dangerous place.[25] But what if one were to attempt to follow the culture and its adjudicating methods, and develop what might be called a Web epistemology? This would be a "webby" means of evaluating which sources would pass muster. How would that differ? What kinds of back-ends and front-ends would be developed?

**Towards Web Epistemologies and Ontologies**

A discussion of Web dynamics and what they may yield might begin by touching on two overarching approaches for making decisions about inclusion: *voluntaristic* and *non-voluntaristic*. (We return later to whether they also achieve fairness, scope of representation, and social-ness.) The voluntaristic approach is one of self-reporting; Webmasters and information recommenders pointing to sites so that they may be placed. Open directories operate in this manner. Calls are made, usually using lists multiply distributed to networks of subscribers, for keepers and contributors to an open directory of one kind or another; for example, dmoz.org. One or more knowledgeable parties in a particular subject area volunteers, or is asked, to maintain a portion of the directory, using low vetting or generally inclusive criteria. In principle, the reporting of sites to the directory is done with the understood goal of inclusion. More recently, online encyclopedias have been collectively authored, as in the open content wikipedia.org project.

With dmoz.org and wikipedia.org in mind, one could characterize the gate-keeping functions of portal directories on a source inclusion spectrum. Open directories would fall to the left of Yahoo!, with the opposite end being an AOL or an MSN, where there are commercial tie-ins and paid placements behind links (and often external hyperlinking policies). Other voluntaristic examples include sites like medialounge.net, where art groups and cultural institutions report themselves (as well as their social links or affiliations) for inclusion in a database that may generate a social network map.[26] In all cases, one volunteers one's site with a classification already in mind.

It is important to complicate the approach slightly by touching on voluntaristic ranking. One's reporting of a site (or a product or a person) may be counted, and the tallies may become sources of ranking. These techniques use registered activities—embedded information—for the purposes of recommendation. For the sake of clarity, if the ranking practice is well known to the surfers and they understand how to boost and privilege, the overall model may still be considered voluntaristic.

Straddling the line between the voluntaristic and non-voluntaristic approaches is the more sophisticated effort behind Alexa's invitation to download its toolbar and the subsequent means by which the Internet archive (and the Way Back machine) have been built. The surfer with the toolbar, installed in tandem with a browser, would contribute knowingly to the Internet archive (archive.org) by allowing the toolbar to record the sites surfed and report them back to the archive. Sites surfed that are not currently in the archive would be visited and indexed later by an archive crawler. Basically, surfers are recommending their surfed sites for archiving, but the sites are not volunteering themselves to be archived.

In a non-voluntaristic approach, there is no self-reporting allowed and inclusion is based on measures of quality of *found* as opposed to self-reported ties. Google works on this general principle (counting large quantities of inlinks). It may be contrasted with the more popular search engines of yesteryear (AltaVista), which ran more on the voluntaristic model—self-reporting of site content in metatags. (We enter into a discussion of some additional consequences of search engine logics as well as collaborative filtering at more length in the next chapter.)

On the basis of the extent to which volunteered information is taken up by the indexers and made available to surfers and searchers, an initial classification of Web-epistemological projects may be made. (See table 1.3.)

Much of the work described in this book follows the non-voluntaristic evaluative model. In adhering to the non-voluntaristic approach, we are endeavoring to maintain some distance from our objects of study. Allowing them to carry on in their everyday capacities is more telling than affecting them with knowledge of our monitoring. We put forward this study with the knowledge that much of the Web has been built on

**Table 1.3**
Web epistemology matrix classifying Web projects on the basis of relationships between the following features: self-reporting (volunteering information to be indexed) and inclusivity of actors (who may wish to be included).

| | Adjudication | |
|---|---|---|
| Collection Method | Inclusive | Exclusive |
| Voluntaristic | Dmoz | Yahoo! |
| | IMD | UK online |
| | | Gezondheidskiosk.nl |
| Non-voluntaristic | archive.org | Google* |

*Ranking logics and indexing methods result in exclusion, as Introna and Nissenbaum have argued.

voluntarism, but we would like to argue that there are occasions and reasons to do without.

One supporting reason for our position is that we are not so naïve to believe our emails, project brief attachments, URL pointers, and software presentations are so compelling as to influence their behavior. In further, realist defense of the non-voluntaristic approach, many have observed that participatory experiments often do not live up to their promises; participatory spaces without participants also depress. But the larger rationale behind the non-voluntaristic approach is that it places the burden of evaluation—and debates about evaluation—on techniques that blame the Web. This overall approach creates a beneficial climate.

Being able to blame the Web would be good news for all the editors and their critics. Concern could be shifted away from editors working with incomplete information, or working under the idea that they must dodge charges of favoritism. With the Web to blame for recommending links, governments, for example, would no longer need to link only to themselves. They would need not worry about a hostile press writing stories about a hyperlink from a government Web site to a call boy network, as in the notorious German case, reported in the *Bild Zeitung*.[27] Concern would be shifted away from commercial editors working on new paid-for-placement schemes and other commercial linking policies. Having blamed the Web, they would be granted relief from *die Nörgler*—those critics and watchdogs toiling on the latest bias exposure cases.[28]

Concern would be shifted away from the editorial practices of even the all-inclusive open directory makers. With the blame placed on the Web, the artist, the alternative Webmaster, or the hotmail scientist, whose paper may have been rejected by arxiv.org on the basis of his or her email address alone,[29] would need not stay awake at night, wondering why the one critic or team of editors did not include the site or paper in the listing.[30]

Even if the terms of debate about source evaluation were successfully shifted from editorial practices to capturing and analyzing Web dynamics, fresh concerns would arise. As many authors have pointed out, the politics and sub-politics of search engines and other evaluative devices remain under-interrogated. Among other problems, these devices may only *appear* to blame the Web in recommending sources as relevant. It is difficult to verify the claim, for the logics are not known in great detail. But once the arguments begin along these lines, the tyrannies of the editors and critics (and debates about them) begin to recede from the picture.

If we are able to shift the debate away from editors to a kind of living Web, with devices capturing dynamics, adjudicating sources, and putting on display other information politics, the political principles still must be taken into account. The outputs must be interrogated according to the info-political system design principles discussed earlier. Perhaps they require amendment. However, I would first like to address the back-end Web and draw up some considerations of what is meant by a living Web, and which sorts of methods and devices already may be capturing it.

To begin, we draw the distinction between information gleaned from the medium—embedded information—and information gleaned from without the medium and put up on the Web—disembedded information. Classic disembedded information, for example, is that which arrives from news feeds from press agencies and is continually mounted on the Web or provided as a stream, often in the form of a ticker, as in BBCnews.com. Similarly, the ever intriguing devices connected to the Internet, with an allotted Yahoo! sub-directory, from coffee and soda machines to clocks, robotic gardens, and Web cams, are disembedded information streams.[31]

The outputs and analysis of classic embedded information, particularly from an info-political point of view, have not seen committed attention from the two disciplines where it may be expected. Internet researchers have long pointed to their initial fascination with tools that show or capture trace routes (the packet trajectories of a message or a page view request through the Internet).[32] The surfer and Webmaster traces left when browsers request pages (hit logs) and when pages refer or link to other pages (referral logs) also have been discussed, but neither ever amounted to the data trove they were once thought to be. Moreover, the scientometric, or Webometric, community, after an initial wax of enthusiasm, has not concentrated its subsequent efforts on score-keeping Web sites or references in discussion lists as serious means of adjudicating either quality or impact of publication.[33] Instead they continue to work with disembedded information. In these areas there is not a Web epistemology under consideration, at least in the terms discussed thus far.

As Rob Kling has pointed out, one of the reasons behind the lack of study of the living Web—capturing and analyzing embedded information for the purposes of adjudication—has been the overall lack of transferability of the arxiv.org model, the physicists' open publishing system which once heralded new Web science.[34] He has discussed the case of the transformation of the idea of E-Biomed—the open publishing system for medical science publications—to PubMed Central, a system without preprints and with considerable lag time between submission and publication. It is a story of the resistance of commercial publishers and scientific

**Table 1.4**
Web epistemology matrix classifying Web projects on the basis of relationships between back-ends and front-ends—what information they capture (information embedded in the medium or disembedded) and whether the information is dynamically generated.

| | Front-end output | |
| --- | --- | --- |
| Back-end source | Static | Dynamic |
| Embedded | Webalyser (site stats) | Lycos top 50, All Consuming[1] |
| Disembedded | | Real-time water,[2] BBC news ticker |

[1] http://www.allconsuming.net. Captures data about the books being mentioned in blogs and lists them according to freshness and frequency of mentioning.
[2] http://water.usgs.gov/realtime.html. Shows real-time hydrologic data from U.S. water stations.

societies to open publishing and new forms of recommendation, where, for example, the combination of paper freshness and recent cross-listings would comprise the principle ranking methods. To the societies and publishers, it may even be dangerous to allow Web dynamics to adjudicate, for they remain untested quality indicators. They are also understudied.

## Information Instruments Doing Politics

This book, among other things, is a contribution to the debate about Web epistemology—the various techniques that capture online (embedded) information, analyze it, and recommend it, often, as is shown, in competition with disembedded information. As mentioned, these techniques fortuitously blame the Web, attempting to leave behind the editors and critics, but also have epistemological and info-political problems of their own. We have entered that debate by building a basic Web epistemology that identifies the features of a living Web, locating the types of devices that may be coming to occupy the term by capturing and analyzing it. It is in the space of devices that capture embedded information, analytically adjudicate, and (dynamically) recommend, that we would like to place our information projects and interrogate our information politics.

In the following chapters, a series of information instruments is put forward that makes strides towards this new Web epistemological practice. The process of thinking through and developing devices that capture Web dynamics on the one hand, and perform an information politics on the other, may first benefit from two definitions. The term *information instrument* is employed here to mean a digital and analytical *means* of recording (capturing) and subsequently reading indications of states of defined information streams. Stream capturing methods are built into the instruments using various programming languages and methods.[35] The interpretations of the streams are designed into the interfaces, where there is an effort to add more depth to the usual flat Web ontologies on offer—to deepen the Web and its devices that usually stream information with vastly different statuses on the same plane.

Indeed, the original way to think about the Web ontologies the devices generate is classical. It has been framed in terms of whether they perform hierarchies in the status of information, whether they classify, and to what effect. For example, the faceted classification system of Yahoo! has a depth to its ontology, whereas the entries in the 2003 *Encyclopedia of New Media* are flatter.[36] (See figure 1.2 and table 1.5).

In pointing to the varying depths of Web ontologies, authors have striven to address one of the original features of the medium, long at the heart of debates and concerns about the overall status of the medium, but, more importantly, debates and concerns about its celebrity. The feature may be called *side-by-sideness*. As the *Whole Earth Catalog* put it in 1992, "the eminent and the crackpot" appear side by side. In our epistemological practice we do not wish to abandon this matter, for it is precisely this medium feature, generated by earlier devices, that may lie behind the expectation that the Web will continue to be flat in the sense of inclusivity and in its scope of representation.

As to the second definition, information politics have a back-end and a front-end. It is thought of in terms of the technical and normative legit-

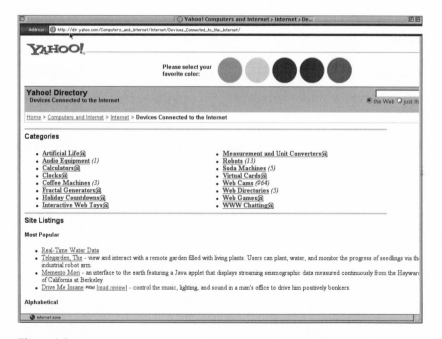

**Figure 1.2**
Yahoo!'s faceted classification of "Devices Connected to the Internet" as an example of deeper Web ontology, captured on February 20, 2003.

**Table 1.5**
Portion of entries list in the *Encyclopedia of New Media* as example of flat ontology.

| | |
|---|---|
| Access | Carmack, John |
| Amazon.com | Carnivore |
| Anderson, Laurie | Case, Steve |
| Andreesen, Marc | Castells, Manuel |
| Anonymity | Cathedral and the Bazaar |
| ARPANET | CAVE |
| As We May Think | Cellular Telephony |
| ASCII Art | Cerf, Vinton |
| Association of Computing | Chat |
| Machinery | Child Online Protection Act & Child |
| Authoring tools | Online Privacy Protection |
| Avatar | Codec |
| | Communications Decency Act |
| Barlow, John Perry | Communitree |
| Berners-Lee, Tim | Community Networking |
| Bernstein v. US Dept. of State | Compression (audio graphic video) |
| Bezos, Jeff | Computer Emergency Response Team |
| BITNET | Computer Graphics |
| Blog | Computer Grids |
| Bluetooth | Computer Music |
| Borg, Anita | Computer Supported Collaborative Work |
| Brand, Stewart | Content filtering |
| Broadband | Convergence |
| Brooks, Rodney | Cookies |
| Bulletin Board Systems | |
| Bush, Vannevar | |
| Business-to-Business | |

imacy of means allowing competition between sources. One may evaluate the extent to which the means as well as outcomes fit with principles of inclusivity, fairness, scope of representation, and social-ness. There will be conflicts when one compromises front-end politics for back-end achievement, as is the current norm on the Web, especially for devices capturing embedded information.

The information politics, moreover, concern a much larger question about the medium more generally. What's the Web *for*, or what could it be made to be for? Should it be made to continue to principally flatten hierarchies of information, itself a highly info-political move? Should it be made to expose, put on display an informational politics? Or, contrarily, should we make the Web compete with press and broadcast media—the very opposite, from an information politics point of view, of convergence? Should it build hierarchies in line with typically mediated versions of events (the Google *terrorism* case discussed above), or should it consciously do otherwise?

With the overall question as to what the Web is for, we enter the debates about (back-end and front-end) information politics by situating our own instruments in them. Here the instruments—and the substance and context behind them—are introduced, one by one. We also discuss the kinds of politics they do, in light of the political analysts' calls for a new public-spirited practice. Finally, we conclude with when and why we part company with those principles, in a Web epistemological practice still very much attuned to information politics.

## Political Instruments for the Web

### The Lay Decision Support System

The first information instrument presented is viagratool.org, the Lay Decision Support System. It is a Web site that provides serious information about a drug, available by searching, form-filling, on-line prescription, e-commerce, and the post. The back-end information stream about Viagra was captured using a manual collaborative filtering technique, the method made famous by the disciples of Vannevar Bush and put into practice on the Web by Amazon.com and others. A group of experts were asked: According to the Web, what is Viagra and who is it for?

As we found with the aid of our group of collaborative filterers, Viagra comes across on the Web as a party drug, with distinct user groups— clubbers, sex tourists, and others—not addressed by the official information providers such as Pfizer and medical industry sites as well as governmental health information providers, including the previously mentioned Ministry of Health initiative Gezondheidskiosk.nl.

Significantly, six months after our finding, press accounts began to appear calling Viagra the new party drug. The research led to two preliminary conclusions, as well as an info-political system design. The first research conclusion is that Web accounts, in pre-dating mainstream journalistic accounts, may serve as an anticipatory medium. This, of course, has far-reaching consequences, and, in the Viagra chapter, we contrast our efforts using the Web as anticipatory medium with some of those who have made similar discoveries at Lycos Top 50, Google, All Consuming, Technorati, and Daypop as well as Jon Kleinberg's work on word "bursts" in blogs as an indication of new trends. We also show the difference between the types of information put on display by capturing search engine query trends and by capturing still other realities Web dynamics have on offer.

The second conclusion also challenges the order of things. If Viagra as party drug is not acknowledged by officialdom, it becomes incumbent upon the information users to exchange information relevant to them, as is often the case on the Internet, especially for medical information, in patient and other support networks. In our instrument, we build upon the more general observation that cohort support networks are challenging expert knowledge and expert-layman distinctions in conventional doctor-patient and doctor-industry relationships. Eventually, the doctor comes to recognize the new learning interface (doctor/Web-aware patient), which is distinct from their usual sources (literature, other doctors, and the medical industry).[37] The instrument, with its Web method of adjudication, is doing the political boundary work that may encourage that shift.

There are two versions of the support system, one for the potential Viagra consumer and another for the often-overlooked second and third parties caught up in "Viagra situations." In the first system, the collaborative filters found and kept information, among other things, about its marketing (and re-selling), its serious harms in cocktail dosages, and insider accounts provided by seasoned lifestyle drug users. The information is displayed on the front-end in a Viagra discourse map with four thought trajectories, each asking whether to consume it, from different angles. Here we borrow information design first developed for didactical purposes at museums and world's fairs.[38] Importantly, the system is *not* a consumer-to-consumer information service or pure cohort support service in the peer-to-peer spirit that the Internet is fostering. Rather, it captures and exposes the range of experiences and arguments about the drug, providing it with a more honest identity. It allows Viagra to become not just the doctor's, the patient's, the industry's, and the regulator's drug, but also the marketer's, the emergency room medic's, the humorist's, and certain other users of Viagra and Viagra substitutes— Web sources also not normally put forward in the doctor's office or on the other official sites. Each could play a part in the Viagra decision. In the second version, we present Viagra situations, quite remote from the placid beach scenes with loving couples found on the Pfizer Web site or a jogging Bob Dole, as seen on TV. In this second version, we move closer still to using the Web as anticipatory medium with the help of unsanctioned information. We first resurrect the second parties in Viagra situations (for example, the prostitute), different from those in "normal, loving" relationships. Finally, we call into existence third party observers—friends and onlookers—anticipating darker Viagra usage scenarios.

In prescribing the sites for information and in anticipating diverse Viagra users as well as Viagra situations on the ground, we perform an information politics. We are showing how sanctioned and unsanctioned information not only may be able to stand side by side (as in the pre-Google days, when an Altavista search for "Shell" would return in the top ten not only the Anglo-Dutch company's site, but also a site parodying company practices), but we are also demonstrating how, in certain cases, Web dynamics and our capturing techniques may allow unsanctioned information to rise comfortably to a new status, with the benevolent effect of anticipating serious situations. In making the case for anticipatory reality instruments such as viagratool.org, we are able to rely on the official Dutch policy of providing information on such banned substances as ecstasy.[39] Thus the Web (with techniques and an information politics) fills in that role not yet assumed by the government and its health portal site.

### The Issue Barometer

The Issue Barometer is more sophisticated. It is an indicator of the pressure of debates around social issues, as may be measured by certain Web dynamics (linking, top-level domain names, and page modification) as well as textual analysis of sites.

To measure the pressure of social debates, we first locate the network around the issues, using special co-link software we developed—a Java crawler and a co-link analysis engine to locate issue networks on the Web.[40] The software, dubbed the Netlocator (and in the later version the IssueCrawler) locates densely interlinked pages on the Web dedicated to issues, given particular starting points. The issue network is displayed (on the front-end) as an astronomical chart or virtual roundtable; the size of the organizational nodes on the map are indications of the number of inlinks each has received from other network actors, and is thought of in terms of standing in the network. The inter-linkings between actors in the debate (the hyperlinks between organizational sites or pages) are seen as social relations, potentially complicating entanglements between the actors seated there. Here the virtual roundtable assumes a depth (in the terms discussed earlier), for, despite all sitting around the same flat table, each actor may have a different standing in the network and may have social affiliations with other actors that have a bearing on what may be said in that company.

In the Issue Barometer gauge attached to the map on the front-end, network activity indicators are shown. These readings of the network are taken from available data per page in the network. For example, the heat of an issue is gauged by measuring the freshness of the actors' issue-specific Web pages in the network. For debate activity we look into the percentage of actors espousing positions (through textual analysis). In the third indicator in the barometer, country-specific data are used to chart levels of territorialization (the involvement of one country versus many countries). The territorialization indicator has been devised especially for the case study at hand.

The case study in question concerns the organization of a public debate on food safety in the Netherlands in 2001, surrounding such issues as genetically modified (GM) food. The Dutch government called for the public debate, which included leading social actors from science, industry, government, civil society, and the citizenry. In 2002 the final report was issued by the government and concluded that the debate was far from successful, citing public disinterest in the issue as well as a lopsided debate, with a series of important actors (NGOs) leaving the forum mid-way.

The question we put to ourselves was straightforward. May the Web (and capturing and analytical techniques) be employed to explain, in part, the failure of classic politics; that is, the national (territorial) public debate? Moreover, can we perform a new information politics that may provide a measure of remedy?

In mapping the food safety debate in the Netherlands, we found that it does not exist, except in the case of certain de-territorial actors brought onto the Dutch food safety debate map by Dutch actors—the Codex Alimentarius Commission and the European Union—actors, crucially, who were not part of the public debate held in the country. In short, the Dutch food safety debate was taking place outside of the Netherlands.

We were able to draw a series of preliminary conclusions from the work. The first is that the Web (with certain techniques) was not only able to show the absence of Dutch debate, but also to point to where the debate was taking place. Indeed, when we analyzed the network of the 15 Dutch NGOs that left the national debate, we found that they were not so much departing the debate, but leading us to it—to a global debate around the Codex, encompassing a wide range of international actors with high levels of heat and debate activity. Cautiously, we put forward the idea that the Web may be able to capture de-territorialization *in situ*, if you will. Finally, we conclude that efforts to stage a national debate—to do classic politics—are often endeavors to re-stage, or re-territorialize, debate, with the Web showing some of the challenges ahead. One of these challenges concerns the extent to which the debate form and format—including the terms—have the capacity to retain those national actors active in the de-territorial arena.

We complicate the performance of classic politics (the national public debate in a building) by showing that the Web tells us that the debate is going on more intensively elsewhere. One could argue that the information instrument points to the political consequences—failed debate, a disinterested public—when one stages classic politics without the aid of the Web or techniques able to capture de-territorialization.

### The Web Issue Index of Civil Society

The Web Issue Index is a variation on the Consumer Price Index that divines (in a sense) the leading social issues and their relative currency over time. Instead of measuring the changing price of a stable basket of goods over time and drawing conclusions about rising and falling inflation, we measure the campaigning behavior of stable sets of NGO actors, drawing conclusions about rising and falling social concerns. In gathering the back-end data, we ask, which campaigns are collectives of NGOs undertaking, and how frequently do the issues change? On the front end, the Index results are delivered in the form of an issue ticker. The stream displays the rising, falling, and stable social issues of interest over time, according to regular queries of two baskets of sources: Seattle protestors and the Dutch Echte Welvaart (genuine welfare) movement. (Further detail is provided in chapter four.) The ticker, moreover, streams issues on three levels, wading from issue, into sub-issues per issue, to a single piece of information per sub-issue that the most NGOs treating that issue are currently pointing to. This may be a document, a statement, a leak, etc.

The value of such an information source is argued from empirical research about the Genoa G8 summit and the anti-globalization movement. In particular, we asked whether the NGOs' portrayals of issues are distinctive enough to warrant a dedicated stream, different from the summit issues portrayed by the printed press (and their digital versions on-line) and by the governmental information providers. We also recognize that there exist a number of dedicated streams to NGO issues such as Oneworld.net, also running on Yahoo! News. Is it necessary to add additional streams, doing multiple site analysis?

Thus here we use the Web to capture informational politics in action (in Castells's sense), providing empirical evidence about the extent of the press coverage (in both online and off-line versions) of NGO issues in comparison to the summiteers's issues. In the argument, we first ascertain whether the press and the governments adequately and rigorously capture the Genoa debate led by the counter-summiteers. To do so, we collect Genoa issue lists from the press, the summiteers, and the NGOs and compare them. We found that neither the governments nor the press scratched the surface of the NGO issues, perhaps because of attention to disembedded information, particularly the more obvious concentration on violence, where the only palpable NGO-related conclusion drawn by the summiteers and covered by the press was to move the next summit to a remote, secure location.

So, here we argue that the Web is substantively closer to the ground— closer, in this case, than the summiteers or the eyewitness reporters from the newspapers (not to mention to the readers of the press and the viewers of protest violence on TV).

Significantly, we also found that, over time, the NGO issues are relatively stable. (This was the good news from Genoa and beyond.) Therefore we need not continually refresh them everyday and compete, for example, with the press as Oneworld.net does, with its daily news from and about NGOs and civil society. This is how we defend our particular issue stream and its politics.

Thus far the Web has been found to be and taken as a valuable collision space between official and unofficial accounts of reality. With collaborative filtering, the network maps, and the issue indexing, the unofficial often sits more easily next to the official situations and events than one would imagine. At viagratool.org, an invitation is extended to address the unofficial realities of the use of a new pharmaceutical product. In the Issue Barometer we question whether national public debates, as well as inter-governmental policy proposals (for example, by the Codex Alimentarius Commission), are addressing the debate on food safety. In the Web Issue Index, we stream alerts about the disconnection between government, the media, and mediated accounts of civil society aims, issues, and positions. In all cases we are increasing exposure to the range of positions and scope of representation of actors without providing flat information.

### The Election Issue Tracker
The Election Issue Tracker charts the press resonance of political party issues in addition to certain NGO issues in the run-up to the national elections. We measure the currency of each political party's platform issues by counting how frequently the issue terms are mentioned in the leading newspapers, using newspaper archives on the Web. To do so on

the back-end, a batch query system is built that can call upon differently constructed newspaper databases (early every morning) and return, simultaneously, the number of issue mentions and the dates per news-paper. Using the familiar information design of a stock market share graph per issue, Election Issue Tracker, on the front end, shows whether and how the political parties' issues resonate in the printed press—how frequently they are mentioned, when and by which newspapers—over the past three months.

Where method is concerned, election issues are first distilled directly from the individual party platforms (culling disembedded information with an eye to terminological specificity, so party issue resonance com-parisons may be made effectively). The specific terms are then fed into the newspaper databases through the batch queries. We show each party's issue resonance as article counts, where one article equals one mentioning.

Election non-issues are also tracked. To do so, we use a stable NGO source basket (from the Web Issue Index with embedded information). Once it is ascertained which NGO issues are not on the platforms of the political parties—the non-issues—we track their media currency in the same manner. We then compare the resonance of issues and non-issues, allowing us to evaluate the extent to which classic informational politics are in play and whether there are alignments between governmental agendas and press resonance, or perhaps between NGO issues on the Web, and the press. Thus we are able to enrich the notion of informa-tional politics by charting such disalignments.

There is a politics built into the system insofar as we are normatively positioning ourselves in favor of elections being about issues, as opposed, for example, to personalities. Principally however, the intent has been to hold up a mirror to party-press relations and pose dilemmas for politi-cal parties (including the governing parties). In a word, the dilemma—the choice between two courses of action, neither of them wholly satisfactory—concerns whether parties will stand by their issues, even if they are not press-friendly. We are also able to chart issue abandonment by parties, seeing whether those issues being abandoned are those that do not resonate in the press.

The effort here is to cross informational politics (in Castells's sense) with the new information politics based on Web epistemological practice being discussed in this book. In the case in question, we watch whether the embedded information may challenge the disembedded over what counts as issues. There were intriguing findings.

We found that there are issues high on certain political party platforms that do not resonate in the press, for example, a European Constitution on the Labour Party platform. Conversely, there are non-issues that also resonate, such as waiting lists in health care. More provocatively, we found in the run-up to the elections that the populist parties that sent shock waves through the Netherlands in May 2002, especially Pim Fortuyn's party, saw their issues resonate most in the press. With that finding in hand, we cautiously attempt to build the case that the press participated, through issue coverage, in the rise of populism. We qualify the statement by saying that the populist issues had the greatest press impact. We also found that parties did not so much abandon issues that were not press-friendly as add the press-friendlier ones to their platforms, thereby resolving the dilemma (and becoming more populist, in issue terms). In the analysis we are able to chart a more general swing towards populism in the Netherlands from the pioneering Pim Fortuyn Party to the press, and subsequently to the establishment parties.

### Towards a Politico-epistemological Practice with the Web

I would like to conclude with the heuristic principles behind the instruments and the extent to which we are embracing or departing from the info-political system design principles previously enumerated by the political analysts. The endeavor is to first take seriously embedded Web information as well as the common Web techniques to capture, adjudicate, and provide recommendations. We are positioning the work here within the space of those devices and techniques that sit on top of Web streams, often cross and/or analyze multiple streams, and dynamically provide them with a depth in the status of the information. However, we shall depart from what may be seen as ludicrous outcomes of the techniques in action thus far—coffee machines connected to the net or Britney Spears appearing as the most sought after item in the engines. These are not the information trends we are after.

While our ontology is concerned with striving for deepness, we are aware of the traditional flatness of the medium—the *side-by-sideness* issue—as a feature that certain public-spirited analysts desire to retain or return to. With them, we have redefined flatness in terms of scope of representation and information exposure, and contrasted that to the practice of traditional informational politics. The aim is to show how the Web may at least enrich how we come to understand when informational politics are and are not at work, as directly in the case of the Web Issue Index as well as the Election Issue Tracker. With the principles of scope of representation and exposure retained, moreover, we feel the Daily Me problems also may be put safely to rest by our particular practice.

By choosing the non-voluntaristic approach to source adjudication, our Web epistemology, however, may suffer from charges of being unfair as well as non-inclusive. After all, exhaustiveness in collection method and inclusivity in adjudication are not adhered to. We do not take the entire Web as our realm of inquiry; we do not offer inclusion to actors who may desire it. (See table 1.6.)

Previously we have raised this issue indirectly in our study—our desire to have the actors carry on unaffected by our monitoring—as well as in the discussion of blaming the Web and how it may provide a salutary means of leaving the debate about the practices of editors behind. To those considerations, more importantly, may be added the fact that unlike the previous device occupying the same space in the matrix—Google—for our devices, the adjudication methods are open. (See table 1.2 and table 1.7.) One knows by reading how the ranking or the high indication is achieved.

**Table 1.6**
Web epistemology matrix classifying the information instruments on the basis of relationships between back-ends and front-ends—what information they capture (information embedded in the medium or disembedded), whether the information is dynamically generated, and whether the information delivered shows depths in status.

|  | Front-end output | |
| --- | --- | --- |
| Back-end source | Flat, Static | Deep, Dynamic |
| Embedded | Viagratool | Issue Barometer, Web Issue Index |
| Disembedded |  | Election Issue Tracker |

**Table 1.7**
Web epistemology matrix classifying information instruments on the basis of relationships between the following features: self-reporting (volunteering information to be indexed) and inclusivity of actors (who may wish to be included).

|  | Adjudication |  |
| --- | --- | --- |
| Collection Method | Inclusive | Exclusive |
| Voluntaristic |  |  |
| Non-voluntaristic |  | Viagratool, IssueCrawler/Issue Barometer, Web Issue Index, Election Issue Tracker |

To put this issue into context, one of the main rationales behind closed logics, apart from commercial secrets, is that knowledge of the logics would enable manipulation. Calls for disclosures of the logics, either by watch groups or by our political analysts, are met with this argument. It results in a stalemate. If, to the analysts, only open logics result in public-spirited information provision, to the logicians it only would result in worse results. (Manipulation routinely sees sites un-indexed—thrown off the Web for a time from a searcher's and an organization's point of view.)

In our instrumentation we have striven to put this particular debate to rest. Significantly, we need not worry ourselves with what may be termed manipulation. Indeed, should an instrument awareness arise that influences behavior and encourages actors and issues to do better in the rankings, the readings become even more telling.

With the exception of viagratool, the instruments have this additional feature, which we wish to add as an info-political system design principle. Thus, in all, we have as our principles and heuristics: scope of representation, exposure to the range of arguments (beyond the highly mediated), social-ness, embedded information, non-voluntaristic collection method, exclusivity in adjudication, deeper ontology, and comprehensible logics inviting what was once termed manipulation. By instruments encouraging what was once termed manipulation, I mean (also as a principle) there is a certain in-built political reflexivity to them. They show the extent to which the actors may be reacting to the dynamics being captured. The clearest case is the Election Issue Tracker, where one is able to notice if parties embrace the press-friendliest issues. Similarly, with the Issue Crawler and Issue Barometer, one may track efforts of organizations intensively networking, and heavily page-modifying, with fresh positions in the debates. In the Web Issue Index, furthermore, one may also monitor NGO efforts to all mount campaigns on the same issues, or campaigns on issues that are suffering from lack of attention. With what normally would be considered cases of manipulation, here political parties' informational politics are displayed. Here, too, issue barometers would register the highest readings and issue indices would witness issue bursts owing to new, collective campaigning behavior by NGOs. Should this occur on the basis of the organizations' independent readings of Web dynamics, let alone from reading the instrumentation described herein (however unlikely), we would not despair in the least. The value of our practice and our information politics would be affirmed.

# 2

## The Viagra Files: The Web as Collision Space between Official and Unofficial Accounts of Reality

### Introduction

This argument begins by touching on medieval practices of knowledge-seeking and how they inform search engine design. Subsequently, one contemporary knowledge-seeking technique based on the old practice—collaborative filtering—is introduced and critiqued. Finally, in the main text are the studies and thinking behind a new instrument, Viagratool.org. The tool has been devised to take into account the old practice as well as the dominant critique of collaborative filtering applications.

Significantly, the instrument is meant to be a reality checker; it shows the extent to which the unofficial accounts of Viagra—what it is, and whom it is for—are challenging Pfizer's official accounts of older men using Viagra to treat erectile dysfunction.[1] The Viagra case study also attempts to put the new medium to a new use: the Web as anticipatory medium. Researchers and I show why the Web may anticipate by demonstrating how Web accounts of Viagra use and users not only enrich and complicate more official accounts by regulatory bodies, the scientific medical industry, and the manufacturer, but also prefigure traditional media discoveries and third party situations on the ground. The thought and technique behind the anticipatory instrument could apply to future products and issues when the Web may be the first to know.

### Knowledge Itineraries and the Web

Medieval scholars, a Czech library scientist recently said, had an intellectual itinerary that was primarily place-based.[2] Their search for knowledge began by knowing where they had to go, but not necessarily what was in store for them once they arrived. They knew the sites (the libraries), and from them they eventually would learn the texts (and the key words). Monks and pilgrims had similar, place-based knowledge itineraries. In one of the final place-based knowledge itineraries in this style, Alexander Csoma de Körös traveled from one site of knowledge to another in search of the origins of the Hungarian people. Instead, he ended up discovering (making known to the West) Tibetan language and literature.[3] Alexander Csoma de Körös is summoned here in an effort to show that mere text-based or key-word queries may result in less telling findings.

A story of medievalist scholarly practice could lead the modern developer of a search logic (or recommender) in at least two directions, one that is traveler-based, or one that is place-based. Here we take up the traveler-based scenario. In that scenario the developer of a search logic would rely on collective traveler knowledge. Sets of itinerant scholars would be followed, and what they have learned at the sites would be stored. To future travelers arriving at those sites would be recommended the collective findings of the fellows that had come previously to all the sites combined. The recommendations made to future scholars could be ranked according to what the most scholars have chosen to keep as knowledge.

Collaborative filtering, a current content recommendation technique, is based on the traveler-knowledge scenario. Those who have searched for a particular subject (or item) and have selected it are providing their selection recommendations—their findings and keepings per search—to their cohorts in the future. Significantly, they are providing these findings to the travelers landing at any of the sites on the trail.

Before beginning a description of the instrument derived from this technique, I would like to lay out briefly the context wherein a critique of collaborative filtering is often situated. The situated critique will help to explain the choice of the different context selected for the employment of the technique. The different context also will aid in explaining why certain web-technique-based knowledge claims about Viagra may be made.

Collaborative filtering—which goes back to the writings of Vannevar Bush[4] and has inspired the idea of consumers' and experts' swapping their search query strings, their preferences, and/or their automated recommendations for money or free products—has been criticised as an ontological and cultural flattener, as a means of placing entities with disparate statuses on the same plane.[5] In discussing Amazon.com's collaborative filtering system, an author wrote in the *New York Times*:

They pair you with another buyer and then propose the other guy's picks to you. . . . It's a little sinister. Your tastes are cloned and cross-referenced so quickly you end up with the sense that idiosyncrasy is impossible.[6]

Note that the criticism does not concern an invasion of privacy as one normally understands it: that is, the matching of people and records *across* databases. One's collaboration in the system does not require furnishing personal data such as name, address, income, or medical records. The system is not recommending on the basis of where you live, or what you earn, together with what those variables could tell the system's users about what you are likely to buy, or why you should be rejected for certain types of insurance. Rather, the criticism is levied on the theft of idiosyncrasy, the difference between you and some guy. At its core, perhaps, the uneasiness rests upon yielding collections of private knowledge to unknown publics, who then act upon your private knowledge without your consent.

Theoretical collaborative filterers solve this problem by referring to an opting in clause—you agree to exchange private knowledge for collective knowledge. (As was mentioned, the bargain is sometimes sweetened with references to a future of earnings, as in contemporary manual or future automated ask the experts schemes.[7]) The theorists also presuppose the existence of a knowledge community with a commons model. In doing so, they attempt to erase certain tragedies of the commons and perfect information, including rivalry, data, and thought scooping.

Another *New York Times* piece took up the problematic effects of perfecting the information stream in science. The criticism is similar to the one above. The piece said that physicists—Web inventors and Web innovators—are becoming wary of a fallowing of the field by the Web.[8] Idiosyncratic avenues of research supposedly are being abandoned because of increasingly perfected information flows.

[I]nstead of fostering many independent approaches to cracking each difficult problem, the Web, by offering scientists a place to post their new results immediately, can create a global bandwagon in which once-isolated scientists rush to become part of the latest trend. . . . "[S]corekeeping" Web sites, which

automatically track the number of times a paper is cited by others, create ...
social pressure against marching to a different drummer.[9]

The scorekeeping Web sites are the culprit in the story of the flattening of difference and the drying up of prospects for radical innovation
previously brought about by relative isolation.[10] I do not wish to evaluate the claim, but only remark that both the marketplace and science
have been held up historically as places that lend themselves to the ideal
of the commons and perfect information in the liberal tradition. For the
market, the perfect information ideal pertains to products and prices.
(Shop AltaVista lays out a price comparison of a goodly number of
Viagra sellers across the Web.) In science, the ideal applies to method
and findings. I would like to introduce a context, however, where neither
the ideal nor the alleged common interest in perfect information
adheres—the underground. The underground is often denied a place
in traditional information streams, unless its relevance can be
demonstrated.

**Exposing Viagra for What It Is**

The intention is not to rehearse claims about the Internet and the Web
as an overall renegade space. (Those Internet days are numbered.)
Rather, we shall attempt to look into the interaction between subspaces—between spaces of the palpably non-authoritative and the palpably authoritative. We do so with a knowledge search exercise—in the
style of the old travelers now with collaborative filtering collection and
evaluation techniques—and inquire into which subspaces come to play
the part of the overall authoritative sources, according to the findings
and keepings of a group of surfer-experts.

The search for information and knowledge exercises described here,
and the ideas for the instrumentation below, were conducted with ten
advanced students at the University of Vienna in September–October of
2000, and again with twenty-five advanced students at the University of
Amsterdam in April 2001. The groups of students were invited to travel,
surf, and forage for information and knowledge on the Internet: that is,
find and determine what is known about a given subject that would
provide answers to particular questions. Upon conclusion of the exercise, the groups were then invited to explain their search for information

and knowledge strategies: that is, how they came to know about the subject, in this case a new drug—Viagra. We are interested in the groups' knowledge acquisition technique, for, we would like to ensure their expert status, beyond that of mere travelers. The advancedness of the students, noted above, is derived from their descriptions of themselves as "webby," alluding to their experience-based capacity to forage and their alleged grasp of different foraging methods. We also briefly tested (or, in fact, hardened) this claim with a search engine tinkering sub-exercise, whereby the groups were invited to compare the same queries across three distinct engines and devise a means (usually by analogy) to describe the different engine logics to a layperson. (So we attempted to create a lay-expert divide, and then make them into experts, at least briefly.) This sub-exercise also provided the groups with a vocabulary to provide a rationale for their search strategy (and, as it turned out, their favorite engine), as we come to below.

What were they after? The lead questions were: What is Viagra, and whom is it for? Viagra was chosen as a subject matter because it is, in some sense, a special Internet phenomenon—a (mail order) prescription drug that is available via the Internet without face-to-face consultation with a physician. The drug's "net flavor" has more features, too. Beyond the new online medical and e-commercial elements, it could be associated with two leading (underground) areas of the net: pornography or sex (Viagra may be thought of as a sex drug) and piracy (Viagra may be had through quasi-legal, unregulated channels, but, at the end of the day, the product is often the genuine article).[11] Does one end up crediting the porn and piracy reaches of the net as knowledge sources or as knowledge pointers when researching Viagra? Do these reaches come to over-determine the substance of the answers to what Viagra is, and whom it is for?

Along the way, we also may be able to say something about the relationship between the online and offline, between incipient web-based knowledge and more traditional knowledge sources. Of crucial importance is the extent to which the medical consumer (patient or non-patient) arrives at the doctor's office with web-derived claims that challenge the official accounts—the doctor's, the medical industry's, or the manufacturer's. (There's also the scenario where they no longer see the need to visit the doctor personally.) Findings such as these would harden claims that the Web knows, or perhaps knows enough, at least for those laypeople making a decision to consume. Indeed, we have dubbed the instrument described below a lay decision support system, in opposition to the expert decision support systems made by the medical industry, employed by doctors, and also put to use by resellers.[12] A light version of such a system may be seen if one were to fill out the online form and attempt to acquire a digital prescription for Viagra.

But beyond the implications for doctor-patient relations and the medical industry, we are mainly interested in the Web's potential as the reality few are acknowledging, or perhaps acknowledging only at a later date. We will attempt to show, indeed, that the Web may be anticipating, and perhaps prefiguring, later acknowledged realities. Thus we shall attempt to demonstrate its potential as an anticipatory medium, at least when comparing Web accounts of what's really going on with more official contemporary and future accounts.

Ultimately, though, we intend to design an instrument that builds on old scholarly practice as well as the new technique (collaborative filtering). To do so, we have the expert travelers set out on a journey, and then we collect all the findings and keepings. Simulating the collaborative filtering technique, we manually chart recurrences of results, and recommend those occurring most frequently relative to all occurrences. We then devise a Web design piece—a new visualization of Viagra—to show what the Web, according to the findings and keepings of the newly appointed experts, says it really is. In doing so, we attempt to move beyond current collaborative filtering recommendation culture—"there's also this that you may be interested in"—to a digital ontology—"you needn't bother looking further."

### Explaining Expert Search Considerations to the Laity

First, the webby takes stock of a range of knowledge search strategies to provide a means of opposing chosen strategies to others, to tailor strategies to search types, and/or to mix strategies in a carefully chosen order. To find out what Viagra's really about, the webby could begin with a favorite search engine; provider or browser default pages or channels; portals; directories; databases; a single, known site; a set of known, trusted sites; sites guessed to be relevant by associative domain name reasoning; discussion lists; or newsgroups. These starting points are discussed briefly, together with their expert commentary on how each should be explained to a layperson, and whether and when each should be employed in a search for knowledge strategy.[13]

According to our experts, the choice of a search engine involves advanced user-based knowledge of the language orientations and especially indexing and ranking logics. National engines, as ilse.nl or aon.at, appear to boost national .nl or .at sites for no other reason than language. By our experts, they were pejoratively dubbed nationalist, and dropped, perhaps too quickly, from all search strategies. It was said that AltaVista, a favorite amongst many non-experts, relies in the first instance on Webmasters' self-descriptions of the contents of sites (metatags). It is via AltaVista, some argued, that one would find the underground cultures—at least, those cultures most likely to build in artful tricks of the manipulators' trade to boost their own sites' rankings across query type (such as listing both authoritative terms and racier key words in their metatags). An identity check for the true underground is the view source feature in browsers, where you can see whether the metatags have been stuffed in this manner. Direct Hit, another site tested by some, relies on a form of collaborative filtering by the masses, whereby those sites returned by the engine that are in turn clicked by the searcher are boosted the next time any searcher queries the same term. This was dubbed a "populist engine." If the logic also relies on metatags, then, it was explained, we could find the most popular underground, if that notion is not too oxymoronic. Google relies on link authority logics and the pointer text written by the Webmaster to describe their outgoing links, so a searcher receives those sites that have the most links with the text that most matches the search query.[14] Fortunately for the understanding of one group of experts, the story had just broken that typing *dumb motherfucker* into Google returned a George W. Bush campaign products site at the top of the rankings. It was surmised that quite a few Webmasters must have used that pointer text to describe the link they made to the Bush campaign products site. Anomalies or telling instances aside, the experts called Google the device most likely to return the official account, or what the majority of webmasters are calling something, on the record. Here we suggested that Google's provision of officialdom accounted for its popularity, and that the arrival of Google accounted for the Web's ascent into reputability, into matching the Web with officialdom, or what some may call the resolution of the real name problem. Previous ideas of the Web as jungle, or rumor mill, coincided with the dominance of AltaVista, the underground's engine, the engine that produced *side-by-sideness* (as discussed in the introduction). Finally, meta-engines, as metacrawler, amalgamate engine returns through triangulation techniques, that is, those returns occurring most frequently in the top sets of the leading engines are boosted in the rankings by the meta-engine. It was pointed out that meta-engines are only as good as the engines whose results they amalgamate. Should a meta-engine be found that amalgamates the official and the unofficial accounts in a sophisticated manner, then we have one for the reality checkers, one where we can watch the competition between the lesser and greater authorities. (A few people in the groups considered such a small software project doable.)

Discussion lists and newsgroups, it was noted, are difficult to characterize generally without caricaturing. Nevertheless, both discussion lists and newsgroups tend to yield informal and tacit knowledge (viewpoints and experiences), often with references given to sources (URLs). Discussion lists, run on email, tend to have at least a quasi-institutional or (amateur) organizational character, if not a formal structure with a vetting threshold to join. Newsgroups, run through usenet, tend to be populated by subject enthusiasts alone, with no threshold to joining or staying on, apart from their newgroups' cultures. Newsgroups have been around since the early 1980s and tend to follow, or at least jest about, an original net etiquette; there are veterans and "newbies." Discussion lists are more recent, and threads of discussion are often broken by event and book announcements by professionals working within the list's subject matter. (Nettime, one major list for net theory and criticism, has attempted to maintain threads by always combining all the event and publication announcements and sending each of them in single postings, or more recently, as a separate list.) In both cases, there are what may be called "list effects;" that is, what one comes to know about a dedicated subject from an .alt or a listserv has much to do with the existing level of discussion and the list's tolerance for questions by the uninitiated. Intriguingly, those who joined or looked up Viagra discussion lists arrived at the unofficial official accounts: that is, they suddenly found themselves among users (and future users) of the product, but also in discussion with a representative of the marketing company that had just been hired by Viagra's maker—Pfizer—to create a new product image and advertising campaign. The previous image, at least in the United States, where the marketing representative is based, revolved around a 70-something Bob Dole, jogging down the beach on television, showing some vigor. Smiles abound. Dole it turns out (in between our two exercises), did a Super Bowl commercial—a major television event in the United States. In it he jogs down the beach again, but upon letting up, he reaches for something else—a Pepsi. This was one context for the marketing representative's query to the list for suggestions about a new look and feel for Viagra. Indeed, reports of this list incident (and the context) to one expert group occasioned many in the ranks to look further into the use of a discussion list as knowledge search strategy, and certain of the more telling findings and keepings are derived from lists. The particular discussion lists queried, some of which are archived on the Web, were said to reveal underground user cultures (as opposed to the user cultures put on display in product testimonials on Pfizer's site). The lists thereby lived up to their most recent touting. They are comprised of anonymous confidantes sharing small truths. Professionals, like the marketer, occasionally break the threads, or even kill lists all together. (The discussion moves elsewhere.)

Portals and directories, like Web sites, are generally heavily edited by the Webmaster or organization. (On these channels, the editorial policy extends beyond the content to the link list, as many portals, borrowing content from elsewhere, only author their link lists; they also may not allow incoming links and may challenge those that do not heed their policy, as discussed in the introduction.[15]) For the purposes of stock-taking of the brief discussion, the experts conceived of portals as issue-oriented (for example, truefood.org was dedicated to the organic vs. genetically modified food issue, though it is authored and branded by Greenpeace) or worldview-oriented (for example, oneworld.net is dedicated to global justice and globalization issues, with only NGO and journalistic pieces available). The experts showed little faith in all-in portals (such as msn.com or startpagina.nl), and only-if-pointed-to interest in news portals (such as BBCnews.com). They also preferred independent portals, which were defined simply as non-commercial. (By independence, for example, was not meant fairness, or representing as many sides and sources to an issue as possible.) They recommended surfing a favorite portal (for example, *Wired News, Slashdot, or Tweakers.net*) on a frequent basis for everyday net-related news, but not to use such a net and tech news portal in the first instance for more specific knowledge-gathering needs. Nevertheless, their guidance about everyday portal consumption could not restrain a few from producing at least one collective finding and keeping from net news. *Wired News* reported that an Israeli scientist was feeding Viagra to daisies, so daisies became one of the answers to the question as to whom Viagra is for.[16] (A debate ensued, however, about whether Viagra was really for the scientist and science. Most concurred, so they were added as well.)

Known sites, trusted sites, and corresponding domain name sites may be used as entry ways in a knowledge search. Going straight to the source on the Web—one way of filling in the notion of disintermediation—often means one of two things, according to the experts. Either one knows where to go without consulting any other site or device—the known site (This idea occasioned the designers of Viagratool.org to make a t-shirt and give it to the Dutch Minister of Education, Culture, and Science; perhaps an advertising strategy could make it into a known site), or one assumes that the leading source on a subject owns the domain name of the subject term. As a search strategy, one opens the browser and moves directly to, in our case, Viagra.com, Viagra.at, Viagra.nl, etc. These are assumed to be the authority on the subject. The authority largely derives from buying power and/or from trademark law, and the idea is that the domain name wars continue to shake out the pretenders from the contenders and owners, with some notable exceptions where trademarks conflict with valid claims, as in the Leonardo case.[17] Choice of authorities may revolve around a preference for .com or .org viewpoints. Viagra.org presumably would be owned by an independent information provider, whilst Viagra.com would presumably be owned by the manufacturer. So this method revolves around presumptions and likelihoods. (At the time of research Viagra.org has been by owned by Cisco discussions, presumably a new initiative by Cisco Systems, though it was offline and we did not dig further. Viagra.com is indeed owned by Pfizer, as is Viagra.nl. (At the time there was no Viagra.at.[18]) Longer domain names including the term Viagra are often encountered, most being unsubtle commercial purveyors of the product.

The designers' choice of the domain name and suffix—Viagratool.org—should be mentioned here as an attempt to compete in the same name space with the more *and* less authoritative; it also bespeaks independence and non-commercialism, without necessarily being fair (as above).

## Viagra According to the Web (Experts)

The findings are split into two generations or temporal realities of Viagra, according to the Web (expert surfers). The first group used their favorite search engines (that is, AltaVista and Google, for the unofficial and the official accounts of Viagra, respectively) and amalgamated the results themselves for the mixed picture. They achieved the mixed realities by concentrating on their chosen site types (independent, etc.), by amalgamating query returns, and finally by looking for recurrences across all the returns. Quickly it was found that Pfizer has lost control of the meaning of its drug. Whether the company has done so consciously, as a matter of strategy, has not been treated, though the presence of the marketer in the Viagra discussion space seems to indicate a company need for strengthening Pfizer-Viagra. All together, Viagra (which from now on refers to a found, mixed reality) is defined as follows:

*Viagra as a Californian drug.* Californian e-commerce sites, under state law, are allowed to issue on-line prescriptions worldwide, and, with this digital prescription, dispense Viagra by mail order to whomever passes the prescription exam and pays for it by credit card. "California-ness" also provides Viagra with both a webby and racy texture. (Early Internet ideology was dubbed "Californian," and Californian may be said to stand for lifestyle experimentation, at least for our experts in Vienna and Amsterdam.)

*Viagra as underground money-maker.* "Money programs" refer to secondary sellers of Viagra. If surfers click through a secondary seller and purchase Viagra on a Californian e-commerce site, the secondary seller receives a percentage of the sales. Often these sites use the technique of doorway pages and load their metatags with terms such as "death by Viagra." Those searching the Web for "death by Viagra" (an otherwise serious concern) are often re-directed to the secondary seller site momentarily, and then auto-re-directed to the Californian seller. (All the middlemen earn a percentage.) The other technique employed by secondary sellers is to craft a homemade Viagra banner ad and place it on a porn site. Clicking this banner ad brings the surfer to the Californian seller. (As mentioned, at this point only California state law was allowing online prescriptions, but sales were being transacted in other (national) jurisdictions. On a UK Viagra mail order site, the buyer must promise to tell his physician that he is self-administering the drug.) Buyers agree to a legal disclaimer that frees sellers of liability.

*Viagra as substitute for natural aphrodisiacs.* On alternative lifestyle sites and their discussion lists, Viagra finds itself entangled in a longer history and culture of aphrodisiacs, with user comparisons between Viagra and its natural substitutes, as well as its predecessors. Here one encounters the most wide-sweeping information about Viagra, Viagra usage, and Viagra lifestyle. Discussions tend to encompass the advantages of mail order purchase of lifestyle drugs among the 30- and 40-year-old set. The sites are favorable toward mail order purchase of Viagra as well as Viagra's natural substitutes. The reasoning the sites employ in defense of mail order and digital prescriptions has much to do with the idea of humans as intelligent agents (one can make one's own decisions) and with confidentiality (one may live in a small town and feel embarrassed to speak about one's problem with a doctor or put one's problems on the pharmacist's counter). Also encountered is the argument that one may not have a medical problem, and thus need not consult any physician or deal with any dispensing pharmacist. Theirs may be an anti-medicalization culture, but here they are putting forward a non-Pfizer-Viagra. We also learn of former Viagra users, those having left the expensive pharmaceutical for natural substitutes, rejoining a now more sophisticated aphrodisiac trajectory.

*Viagra as smile.* As expected, many people have crafted somewhat lewd and playful portrayals of the hazards of Viagra. Most cartoons revolve around death by Viagra and the embarrassing state of the corpse upon discovery by the authorities. Bob Dole appears as well; a mere mention is humorous. Also the name Viagra—life, vigor, vivacious, Niagara Falls—is enough to bring on the smile. The humorist also appeared, if implicitly, on the *Wired News* site with a story of Israeli scientists feeding Viagra to daisies and finding that consumption in certain quantities, under certain conditions, delayed their drooping. Science became implicated in Viagra as smile.

*Viagra as unknown emergency room predicament.* Health warnings begin with the "Dear Doctor" letter written by a Pfizer physician to the medical community. This letter, appearing most readily on the U.S. Food and Drug Administration site (http://www.fda.gov/medwatch/safety/1998/viagra.htm) and remounted in numerous other (highly ranked) places in official and underground cultures, details to paramedics and emergency room doctors the hazardous combination of Viagra and nitrates, perhaps the most well known of which goes by the name poppers. Taken in combination with poppers, Viagra may induce a stroke. It is also written that emergency room staff often administer a nitrate to stroke victims, and that they should be aware that the introduction of a nitrate (to a stroke-by-Viagra victim in an emergency situation) could prove fatal.

The users of Viagra, broadly defined, then are Californian companies with virtual doctors, web money-makers with referral Web sites and/or banner ads, former and future natural aphrodisiac consumers, humorists (and, by extension, Bob Dole, Israeli scientists, and daisies), and popper users now in emergency rooms. The curiosity of this list should not take away from the starkest finding of the amalgamations: Viagra, to the Web (experts), has become a lifestyle drug for men in their twenties, thirties, and forties, to be obtained from virtual doctors, having had referrals from death by Viagra search engine queries or from banner ads on porn or racy sites. Having had scant previous exposure to the Viagra phenomenon, the Austrian group was surprised to learn that Viagra was developed and marketed by Pfizer as a drug to treat erectile dysfunction (ED) in active senior citizens. (Significantly, many were sure it wasn't a treatment for a dysfunction per se, but rather an arouser or stimulant.) Part of the official ED reality was indeed encountered and retained; the

Californian dispensers, such as kwikmed.com, carry the Pfizer take and look on the drug, with scientific terminology (Viagra is the trade name for *sildenafil citrate*), usage prerequisites and guidelines, mention of approval by the U.S. Food and Drug Administration, the light blue medical appearance, a beach scene and similar elements. But our experts are introduced to this account only with the knowledge that it appears to be a front of a kind for all the other users who are redirected there— the former natural aphrodisiac enthusiasts, the current popper users, and experimenters of various stripes. (The daisies, the Israeli scientist, and science, after all, could be just the tip of the iceberg, as the Dutch group found.) They also note immediately that Kwikmed is also offering treatments for obesity and hair loss, sure signs of a lifestyle drug company and midlife crisis. The most official source—Pzifer—only survived expert vetting by having had its "Dear Doctor" letter to medics (and the FDA) republished and linked to far and wide. Furthermore, perhaps the most intelligent discussion is found on the yohimbe pages at the natural aphrodisiacs center (http://www.yohimbine.org), a side-by-side site (like Viagratool.org) where the downsides of Viagra are discussed in user comparison stories next to the low moods experienced after use of yohimbine. (Incidentally, the Dear Doctor letter is not on Pfizer sites, which perhaps explains the company's absence otherwise.) Similarly, the government only arises by carrying the letter to the emergency room medics.

Before discussing the strategies and the findings of the Dutch group, I would like to move now to the first visualization of the findings—the initial lay decision support system, also known as Viagratool.org (see figure 2.1). In the center is the sentence from yohimbe.org: "Viagra is a lifestyle drug like a Porsche is a lifestyle vehicle"—the leading (recurring) unofficial claim, now made official by our experts. It also was partly confirmed, or at least made more comprehensible, by the Pfizer Dear Doctor letter. This statement sums up the main finding regarding the other Viagra and the other Viagra user, our competing reality conjured by the Web.

In all, the interface is meant to be an alternative to lists of search engine returns or collaborative filtering returns. It is laid out in a spoke-and-wheel design, with each spoke representing a thought trajectory. One

## viagratool.org

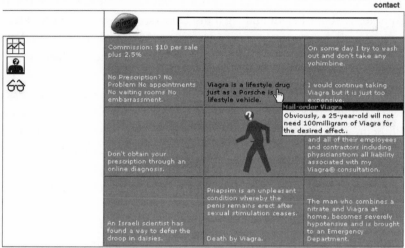

Figure 2.1
Viagratool.org, version one, with method and design considerations. Graphic by Marieke van Dijk, Anderemedia.nl, with the Govcom.org Foundation, Amsterdam.

trajectory concerns the Viagra business on the Web, from sellers to the incentives for resellers, with exact dollar figures of the cuts to be taken. Another is about health and legal disclaimers, whereby thoughts extend from the disclaimer to the emergency room. Yet another spoke is about natural alternatives, their users, and their lifestyles (one of which is from a discussion list). Here one comes into contact with the company the drug keeps. Speaking of a Viagra alternative, for example, one user writes: "On some days I try to wash out and don't take any yohimbe. I'll be in a bad mood, and not very creative, but the following night, I will usually sleep eight hours, and be a much heavier snorer."[19] Finally, the last thought trajectory concerns non-human users, such as science and daisies, where thoughts may lead to prescriptions for non-humans and to basic ethics.

Each of the statements on the interface provides a foretaste of what's really going on with Viagra. Rolling over the statements or questions brings the tool user to one answer: that is, rolling over "An Israeli scientist has found a new use for Viagra" shows "He feeds it to daisies." According to the experts, all that is most significantly known on the Web about what Viagra is and whom it is for is there in a glance. To view the source of the known, one clicks on the statement and moves to the Web page. (They are deep links.)

In contrast to the Austrians, the Dutch group began the exercise with some foreknowledge of Viagra culture, if only through a very recent article in a leading Saturday newspaper magazine, which read that on the Internet "Viagra is being promoted as a designer drug."[20] Most significantly, but unbeknownst to the researchers at the outset, was the series of stories that had broken about Viagra use by ravers and clubbers. It was reported that carousers from Hartford, Connecticut to Dublin, Glasgow, London, and Copenhagen were taking Viagra, not with poppers (as in the Dear Doctor letter from Pfizer), but after ecstasy. Viagra and its users were expanding from seniors on medical treatment to stimulated recreationalists on methamphetamines. (More non-humans were encountered, too.) Now the first Viagratool.org would become a pre-history of Viagra's evolution.

The Dutch group followed a similar search engine strategy as discussed above (the competition between the underground and above ground), but concentrated in the first instance on the question, who is it for? From those answers, they derived their definitions of what Viagra is. To the experts, Viagra, in April 2001, was for the following users (in order of recurrence):

*Party people, clubbers, and ravers,* at places like The Complex in London, at the the Arches and the Tunnel in Glasgow, and in unnamed clubs in Dublin, Copenhagen, Sydney, and on the West and East coasts of the United States, see Viagra as a means of achieving erection after having taken ecstasy and/or speed. In Britain it goes by the street name poke. "The seasoned dealer claims he earns 5,000 pounds ($9,000 US) per week peddling Viagra tablets at 40 pounds ($70) a pop."[21]

*Older men* make a comeback, but as patients about to have sex. These accounts describe the ED target group and placid beach scenes reappear.[22] It is emphasized that these patients know they will be having sex within an hour. The effect may last up to four hours.

*Women,* those with a thin uterus lining and those looking for a stimulant, make their first appearance. A variety of studies were performed. The one most frequently encountered, in Boston, concluded that it had a desired effect on 25 percent of women "as long as the situation is one she would normally find enjoyable, arousing, and emotionally fulfilling."[23] (Previously, official accounts insisted that the drug was only for men.) The experts began to be slightly troubled by Viagra as stimulant upon reading such quotes, where unstated other situations (unenjoyable, non-arousing, emotionally unfulfilling) come across just as clearly, they said.

*Giant Male Chinese Pandas* have been given Viagra. We learn that Viagra is the latest in a long line of reproductive treatments of pandas. The most frequently encountered quotation, from a Sichuan zookeeper, reads: "We tried to give them Chinese medicine in the mid-1990s. As a result, the sex drive of the pandas did improve but they also became hot-tempered and attacked the females. That obviously wasn't so good and we had to end the experiment."[24] Viagra, fit into a lineage of zookeepers' reproductive efforts, becomes something given to users. The Israeli scientist, who no longer appears, comes to mind, but his tests become comparatively innocuous. (The previous relationship between animals and Viagra was different. It was once thought that the availability of Viagra would stem the slaughter of endangered species—ingredients for natural aphrodisiacs.[25])

*Gay men*, now that pre-histories of Viagra as party drug begin to be written, play the part of the proto-alternative users (for the first time). In the same stories, one reads that it should not be taken in combination with an anti-HIV drug.

Foreshadowed by the Austrian findings, in the Dutch findings Viagra, overall, has become far less a medical treatment than a recreational stimulant for party people. The beach faded to darker, late night scenes and later to enclosed zoo settings. Recall that the conventional alternative users in the Austrian findings were aphrodisiac recreational users, with experience and comparative research behind them. (Older hippies on the island of Ibiza come to mind.) They have left the picture. Intriguingly, we also recall from Austria that these users were beginning to find Viagra too expensive, and leaving the pharmaceutical anyway. Apparently they had been accustomed to frequent use, and Viagra didn't fit with the aphrodisiac user culture. Pornographers, whilst encountered, were not kept by the experts, as referrals for the drug were often from advertising around lifestyle stories (clubbers, gays, *Salon* magazine) and sponsored links on search engine return pages. To obtain the drug, the pornographer is no longer among the notable passage points. Thus our underground also has improved its standing.

Pfizer, for the first time, makes the system, in a FAQ page introducing Viagra with the quotations: "So with Viagra, a touch or a glance from your partner can lead to something more;" and "Take Viagra about one hour before engaging in sexual activity. For most patients, beginning in about 30 minutes and lasting up to four hours, Viagra can help you get an erection if you are sexually excited."[26] In the same FAQ, it is pointed out the sexual excitement is a pre-condition for viagric erection, and Viagra helps only with the erection, not with the excitement. Here the Viagra user becomes a patient in need of excitement and about to have sex. (Without the patient tag, our experts chose to call these users men who know they will have sex within an hour, and then for a long time.) In all, the experts have arrived at three, perhaps four, non-patient user scenarios, with the non-patient predominating over the patient. Viagra, as indicated above, also has darkened. With our new Viagras we learn that women are emotionally unfulfilled, mellowed ecstasy users are seeking a sharpener, pandas are hot-tempered, and anti-HIV drug users are excluded.

For the visualization—the second generation of Viagratool.org—we have chosen the "many faces of Viagra" approach, faces indicating our new users, and by inference the new Viagra's: the clubber on ecstasy; the older, expectant male (patient); the emotionally fulfilled but sexually non-aroused woman; the formerly hot-tempered panda; and the gay man who is not taking an anti-HIV drug. (The gay man may or may not be a person living with HIV-AIDS.)

In the design, the name space argument (as above) still applies; we remain in the Viagra name space, with the .org outlook defined by our experts: independent, but perhaps also unfair, at least to the tastes of the old officialdom, we presume. But in the design, the competition with the official account now becomes a little less subtle than in the first generation of Viagratool.org. At Viagra.nl, the official Dutch Pfizer site, a set of faces appear showing the official target group, largely men over 45, maybe over 50, and not older than 70. But there are new faces to be shown now. Pfizer-Viagra is also becoming more youthful, Web-Viagra more so.

To be clear, we have no intention of rogueing the Dutch Pfizer site, that is, parodying it by using a similar look and subtly changed faces and text, in order to furnish a social (Web) critique. In fact, we (normatively) prefer their users, men who are part of loving senior couples about to embark upon on a little experiment or on a late afternoon outing to the beach, toes in the sand. Word has reached us from the underground, however, that enriches and complicates the official account. Our newly appointed experts have deemed this word of greater value than the previously official account. They report that Viagra has long been what it never was.

## viagratool.org

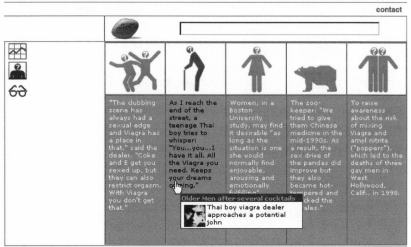

Figure 2.2
Viagratool.org, version two, with design considerations and main finding. Graphic by Marieke van Dijk, Anderemedia.nl, with the Govcom.org Foundation, Amsterdam.

### Bringing to Life New Viagra Subjects and Situations

There are stark realities on the Web.

A 52-year-old Illinois man with episodes of chest pain and a family history of heart disease died of a heart attack in March 1999 after buying the impotence drug Viagra (sildenafil citrate) from an online source that required only answers to a questionnaire to qualify for the prescription. Though there is no proof linking the man's death to the drug, FDA officials say that a traditional doctor-patient relationship, along with a physical examination, may have uncovered any health problems such as heart disease and could have ensured that proper treatments were prescribed.[27]

In the Spring of 2001 a search in AltaVista for "death by Viagra" returned, in the top ten, one media story (not the one above, which is a government media story), four jokes, and five Viagra resellers. The same in Google returned an FDA death count from 1998, one medical center report, one media story and seven jokes, two of which redirected the surfer to a reseller. "Viagra death" in AltaVista produced the same results, while in Google it returned fewer jokes and more media stories (again, not the one above).

The solution to this (automated) search engine problem put forward by commercial and non-commercial entities alike has been the human-vetted directory. Indeed, a few of the major engine-portals have moved to this model, and the open directory project (dmoz.org) is a leading version. Operating with different motives, the latter is meant to be more inclusive, fairer.

In any event, the commercial directory brings the user to the more official accounts (and places to order the drug), whilst the non-commercial directory has official stories, user tales, quality lists (drugs that interact with Viagra[28]), and places to order the drug. In all directories encountered, Pfizer is ranked first. The norm for the order of the directory returns is as follows: Pfizer, then the government, then buy here, and perhaps some discussion. The media, the yohimbe alternative aphrodisiac center, the money programs dollar figures, the pandas, the daisies, the Boston women, the ravers, poke, and the "Dear Doctor" letter are left out. We are faced with the curious situation where our experts do not agree with the expert human arbiters of the Web. Experts often disagree, but what's going on here?

We are not concerned; in fact, our hearts are gladdened by the contribution made by our experts. From the outset the point of the exercises has been to introduce findings of a method based on an old practice (scholar travels), and situate that method in a new context for the travelers (the underground). We have been interested in whether the underground survives a competition with the above ground accounts (and vice versa). And, finally, we are interested in what remains from the scholar-travelers' encounter with the interaction between the polar extremes—the returns of the automated and the returns of the human. So our experts are the creators, and arbiters, of human-engine interaction.

We are not in disagreement with either of the extremes per se, human or engine. In league with the engines, we do not take fairness as an *a priori* criterion of what is presented as leading findings. We are following the non-voluntaristic approach, discussed in chapter one. In league with the directories, we would like humans to decide. Above all, however, we would like to think that there is more to be decided, after the engines and after the humans have had their says.

What has been decided? Judging from our expert recommendations, the underground has had an airing, and Viagra leads a richer, more youthful and experimental life than it is granted by the doctors, the medical industry, and the manufacturer—all of whom retain Viagra as a prescription drug for a patient with a medical ailment.

One official account continues to hold sway: the Pfizer target group—older men with the small problem (afflicting about 30 million Americans, it is said)—is to follow the Pfizer guidelines. Especially if one is not fit, see the doctor; out of town, if necessary. But in the current (official) situation, all others appear to be allowed to experiment freely after ticking off the right boxes in the questionnaire and giving a name, a credit card number, and an expiration date. Only the emergency room medics may not allow free experimentation, but their entry is rather late in the game.

The underground accounts, now above ground and resting, as far as they are concerned, quite easily next to the officials', do not allow the rest to experiment freely. Depending on the Viagra in use, beware of emotional un-fulfillment, hot-temperedness, mood swings, and blues of the alternatives. Forty pounds is too expensive for poke. It may be worthwhile to watch who is taking it, for they know they will have sex within an hour. (They're in certain clubs.) Porn was once the place for referrals; *Salon* magazine now does it (which may make it more respectable). Note the legal disclaimer. These and others, read directly (instead of between the lines of the official accounts), are the situations the Web aids in anticipating. The Web, the technique, and the tool are teasing them out.

Finally, the Web has introduced not only the many new first parties (users) and certain second parties (the partners), but other new third parties, too. There are third-party places—the lifestyle center and the emergency room—and there are new third party observers—the ethicist concerned with non-humans (and humans), the friend (a sort of designated driver of the situation), the contemporary Viagra history-writer (not to be left to the company or to the humorist alone!), and the Viagratool-maker—making new identities and situated realities official and serious. Perhaps this is what could be meant by the Web's capacity, with techniques capturing embedded information and adjudicating sources, to bring to life a competing information politics from below.

# 3

## Mapping De-territorialization: Classic Politics in Tatters

### Introduction

Over the past decade Northern European and other countries have witnessed the upsurge of organized national public debate on leading social issues. Whilst viewed by government as a remedy for the disconnection between citizens and the political process, the national public debate methods and techniques have yet to take into account one of the leading explanations for such disconnected-ness: the challenges posed by de-territorialization.

With the aid of the Web, one may capture de-territorialization *in situ*; that is, the displacement of issue-making, of relevant social groups, and of decision-making input to networks, actors, and positions outside the national institutional framework. Once a de-territorialized issue has been located, the organization of national public debates becomes a matter of re-territorialization, with the Web providing indicators of the challenges ahead.

This chapter takes up recent efforts made to stage a national public debate on food safety and genetically modified food (with experts and laypeople), and how the Web may aid in showing when and why such re-territorialization moves may fail. To do so, we follow, map, and visualize the national and international circulation of the issues of food safety and genetically modified food (the networks, actors, and positions). In the government's endeavors to import the issues into a public debate format in the Netherlands, we watch the collision between issue networks and more conventional democratic forums (classic politics), and ultimately the "crisis of democracy" as a problem of the format of a national public debate.[1] Government's main reservations and findings—disinterested publics, eyes glossing over carefully codified food labels in supermarkets, the departure of 15 leading social groups to another debate (and eventually to a different building filled with de-territorialized issue network themes and players)—lead us to question how the Web may come to reveal and also accommodate forms of democratic practice.

### Public Debate: Classic Politics in Action

Dutch public debate as a form of democratic practice is often introduced as a national cultural commitment to the Polder model, perhaps best understood as a description of a process by which broad social consensus appears to be reached around a policy. The consensus subsequently forms a leading rationale behind the justification of legislation. In the literature even more attention is paid to the latest techniques of public debate—the Dutch formats in relation to other national or regional types (Dutch public debate in relation to Minnesotan citizen juries, Danish citizen panels, British and Danish consensus conferences, German *Plannungszellen*, etc.), as well as the latest format innovations within the Netherlands itself (for example, interactive policy-making and policy exhibitions).[2]

Much less emphasis is placed, however, on the preparatory work behind at least three rather crucial features of public debate organization: choosing the theme and the questions of the debate (and the scope of their "debate-ability"), ascertaining the extent of ongoing *social debate* prior to the organization of a *public debate* (and the inclusion or exclusion of the themes, questions, and players in the ongoing social debate), and, finally, selecting the key players and calling forth citizens to stage the practice. In the following the questions of the extent of the ongoing debate, as well as the selection of the debating parties, are considered in a comparison between ongoing social debates and the official public debate around genetically modified food debate in the Netherlands and elsewhere in 2001–2002. The debate framings—the extent to which the points of departure are overly narrow—are also touched upon.[3]

To begin to arrive at answers to the questions, one of the leading Dutch traditions in the preparation of public debates is reinstalled in the age of the Internet: the preparation of *sociale kaarten* (or social maps). These days mapping a debate, with the aid of certain Web techniques, metrics, and indicators, allows one to come to understandings of the location, level, and intensity of territorial debate around an issue and make comparisons with the de-territorial. Once the issue network(s) are located on the Web, they are queried for properties related to the pressure of (national) debate; that is, the temperature (how "hot" the issue is), activity (the percentage of actors taking positions), and the territorialization (where the actors in the issue network are located). We measure the collective activities of the actors in an issue network to ascertain where debate, and what kind of debate, may be taking place.

In all, the research findings point to the difficulties in staging a national public debate if careful consideration is not paid to the national parties already active in de-territorialized debates.

### Debate Mapping: Historical Interlude

One may situate the issue and debate-mapping work discussed below within the context of other efforts to graphically represent debates around issues, or make issue maps. (We refrain from discussing the richer lineage of sociograms, covered elsewhere.[4]) As a preface to this brief historical interlude, it is important to point out that the following may appear as illustrations of a series of generations of issue map-making, moving from older, simpler issue maps to more recent, complicated ones. Suffice it to say here that all of these generations are still active today. In a contemporary study of issues and their representations, one may find two-column tables of arguments for and against a position, multiple-column tables with representations of actors and positions, and tree-like and other structures showing actors, positions, and relationships between actors and positions.

There are numerous ways to graphically represent an issue, with one of the simplest being a two-column table of the pros and cons, or costs and benefits. Table 3.1 is one such example. It is one of many characterizations of the Channel Tunnel debate in Britain over the years, this one from 1906.[5] Note that the debate may be summarized as a set of arguments, for and against, without recourse to the actual actors and interests involved. This is actor-free debate representation. The interpretation of the map by its analyst is at the bottom of the chart. To the

**Table 3.1**
British Channel Tunnel Debate, 1906.

| Pro | Con |
| --- | --- |
| Scientific | |
| 1. Geological conditions safe. | 1. They appear to be safe. Nothing but the completion of the work can prove this. |
| Military and Naval | |
| 2. Easy Government control by redoubt G and guns of Dover Castle; electric button floods tunnel in three minutes; moreover French are willing to build approach to tunnel in a position commanded by guns of British Fleet | 2. This control dependent on *human*, and therefore fallible conditions. The capture of Dover, though not probable, is possible, for all is possible in war. |
| 3. Food supplies guaranteed in time of war. | 3. = Objection 2, *plus* fact that the cession of the tunnel would be the first thing to be demanded after a disastrous war. |
| 4. When aeroplanes come into existence, five or six tunnels will make no difference. | 4. Aeroplanes in war as yet hypothetical. In any case, Great Britain would lose its insular position; the army would have to be greatly strengthened to defend the tunnel, or recover it if lost, and the whole conditions of British defence would be altered. |
| Commercial | |
| 5. (a) Immense development of trade when Paris and Brussels are brought within four and five hours of London; (b) Probable passengers alone estimated at 1,500,000 and profits £1,250,000 per annum. | 5. (a) Certain trade may develop— for example, small perishable articles, but not heavy and bulky goods, which will still go by water, the cheapest means of transit. Shipping and other industries may be injured; (b) Questionable whether passengers will flock to a tunnel where they may be drowned, blown up, or asphyxiated in the space of a few minutes. |

**Table 3.1**
(continued)

| Pro | Con |
| --- | --- |
| 6. (a) French gauge of Northern Railway a mere fraction of an inch wider, and rolling-stock of every country, except Russia and Spain (whose gauges differ materially from the British) available; (b) gradients easy. | 6. (a) French gauge and rolling stock different from British, hence breaking bulk will still be necessary; (b) maximum gradient, 1 in 55, is very stiff for fast traffic. Compare Simplon, 1 in 145, and St. Gothard, 1 in 172. |
| 7. The international company promoters are all well-tried men, and they have the profitable example of the Swiss tunnels before them. | 7. Such an enterprise should not be in the hands of a company at all, for British interests may be voted down. If built at all, it should be a Government undertaking. Moreover, the Swiss tunnels are not to the point; they do not alter frontiers. Again, good dividends are by no means the main point to consider. Better commence a system of train ferries (as in USA). They could be ready in two years, and would cost less than £1,000,000 each. |
| Social<br>8. It will improve the *entente cordiale*. | 8. It will have no effect on the *entente cordiale*, which does not depend on propinquity. Moreover, France is not the only nation on the other end. A surplusage of cordite at our end would be always necessary to counterbalance a shortage of cordite at the other! |

"The student of the hidden agenda might well be tempted to count the number of words in each column to see where this 'neutral' author's sympathies lie."
Source: W.E. Marsden, 1990. Marsden's source for the debate table is E.R. Wethey, 1906.

analyst, the debate cartographer is thought to be against the Channel Tunnel because of the quantity of words under the cons listed.

To an issue depiction, as the one above, one may add actors by name and/or by sector. Table 3.2 is an actor standpoint map (or table) by issue, made in the early 1980s in the Netherlands, at the time of the great energy debate, known nationally as the "broad societal discussion."[6] The tradition of *sociale kaarten* derives in large part from this nuclear energy debate. The technique employed to gather the data is straightforward. On the basis of consultation with established sectoral players in Dutch society and subsequently a questionnaire, the actors and their standpoints are mapped against one another.

Looking at the table in more detail, the government—the debate organizer—is seeking manageable input to the nuclear energy debate by soliciting institutional views (from establishment as well as alternative organizations) on how energy should be produced in future; that is, by the use of coal, oil, natural gas, sustainable energy sources, etc. The government has set itself three scenarios of usage per energy source, and asks all of the organizations whether each should be eliminated, modestly expanded (for a short period of time), or expanded, perhaps to the exclusion of others. The tables show which actors (in acronyms) are in favor of which scenario, per energy source. Eventually one may count positions per policy option, drawing conclusions on the basis of majority position-taking for a particular mix of energy sources for a future national energy policy. One also may subsequently contact sets of divided parties for a debate, providing the map (or table) as introductory input.

Not so unlike the UK online Citizens' Portal discussed in chapter one, Dutch *sociale kaarten* are edited governmental debates—who's who guides to the issue-makers and their positions according to government.[7] They are meant to provide an overview of the leading parties and the leading parties' viewpoints to a debate around an issue. Significantly, however, they are mainly impositions of actors onto positions—an analytical approach that characterises viewpoints into a narrow framework to make the debate neater. In this sense they are for late policy-making: determining directions after the debate agenda is already set. Indeed, critics of this general Dutch approach often point out the extent to which prior debate framings pre-determine outcomes. (This is also the case in the public debate on genetically modified food, as we note below, where the governmental framing occasioned leading Dutch NGOs to leave the public debate and begin their own counter-debate.)

More recently, debate mapping is concentrating on emerging issues and networks around issues, where the question of organizing a formatted public debate is left open at the outset. In arguing for or against particular forms of democratic practice, one of the normative rationales behind locating emerging debate—positions, actors, locations—is to forestall the critique of pre-given outcomes mentioned above. Perhaps more significantly, one may undertake a comparison between those groups invited to the public debate and those groups already in a debate elsewhere, and note the extent to which the positions being taken in the debate elsewhere depart significantly from the framings of the national public debate. In the following we shall elaborate on techniques that capture and read emerging debate, where potentially newly relevant actors and agenda points are extracted from a sea of issue and debate information on the Web. We also pursue the more important idea that national public debates these days are actually attempts at re-territorializing larger social debates.

## The Web as Source for Dynamic Debate Mapping

Nowadays issue maps may be created by capturing certain data streams available on the Internet, with less editorial input than in the other techniques (and fewer debates about the imposition of positions onto actors and other practices of debate management by editors). In contrast to the actor standpoint maps introduced above, here the techniques are employed to capture Web dynamics that point to emerging issue networks, where we query the extent of the debate. In other words, techniques are employed that allow the actors to lead us to other actors, to positions as well as the relative presence of actors and positions in (national and international) networks.

Figure 3.1 is a representation of the issue network around HIV-AIDs in Russia, found with the aid of the *Netlocator*. (This example has only actors, and no positions.) In order to locate an issue network, leading organizations debating the issue are first identified. This is accomplished initially by choosing entry points to the issue—the organizations one expects or finds to be engaged in the issue and involved in the debate.

**Table 3.2**
The Question of Oil from the Great Dutch Energy Debate, 1983.

Positions of Institutional Representatives on the Use of Oil.
Question 4a: *Which of these positions do you find the best?*
Position 1: The use of oil must be severely reduced.
Position 2: The use of oil must be limited.
Position 3: The use of oil must not be limited.

|  | Position 1 | Position 2 | Position 3 | Other Position |
|---|---|---|---|---|
| Employers' Groups |  | KNOV, KNO, MU, (VNO), (KCW) |  |  |
| Employees' Unions | FNV | CNV |  |  |
| Other Employer/ Employee | VEWIN | CECOIN, CB, NEI, NIVE, NVB, VNCI |  |  |
| Energy Sector | AP | AKA, VDEN, NAF, NEOM, NeA, EA, EI ENCI, NC, ICI, UKF, GB, NHBe, HH, DPN, Ho, Par, CE, HM, VEGIN, MKCB, (LEK), (VNA) |  | (SEP) |
| Transport Sector | LH-Schiphol IWW, ENFB | KNAC, VeCNV, FS, KLM, CBRB, LH-R'dam, RAI, (ROVER) | NOB, NISS, BOVAG, NLR, KVO |  |
| Agricultural Sector |  | ULG, NCR |  |  |
| Built Environment Sector | PTB | NIVAG, BNS |  |  |
| Science and Technology Sector |  | HMW, KIVI-kern., KIO, MC, SC,(TNO) |  |  |
| Environmental Sector | WNF, VBIJ | LVBW |  |  |
| Welfare Sector |  | NOW, LCGJ | NJJ |  |

**Table 3.2**
(continued)

Positions of Institutional Representatives on the Use of Oil.
Question 4a: *Which of these positions do you find the best?*
Position 1: The use of oil must be severely reduced.
Position 2: The use of oil must be limited.
Position 3: The use of oil must not be limited.

|  | Position 1 | Position 2 | Position 3 | Other Position |
|---|---|---|---|---|
| Health Sector |  | NKI, NV-Rad. |  |  |
| Lifestyle Sector | HV | DISK, GV, PIK, SELK, VLRJ, WRvK-Ha, WHGEl.,WH W-As. |  |  |
| Women's Sector |  | VAC, HVG, VHVF |  |  |
| Third World Sector | SWD, GEMCO | BMB, EC, TEMID |  |  |

(–) Institutions which did not fill in the questionnaire, but have made their positions known in a statement or letter.
*Source*: Stuurgroep Maatschappelijke Discussie Energiebeleid, 1983, 138. Translation of questions and terms by the author; acronyms of organizations remain in Dutch.

One may choose entry points in any number of ways: for example, by asking an expert whom he or she believes is relevant in the debate, by reading a leading news piece and choosing the sources cited in it, by snowballing from one or more leading parties to the debate (through link lists or journalistic methods), or by intuition. (A longer list of these entry point heuristics was provided in chapter two.) A combination of methods would allow for an aggregation of the issue networks revealed by different methods; one could triangulate the results and seek the most authoritative network by checking the frequency of appearances of a site per network. Taken together, the most frequently appearing sites would constitute the most authoritative issue network according to this particular method.[8] One may also restrict one's entry points to a particular country, as we do below.

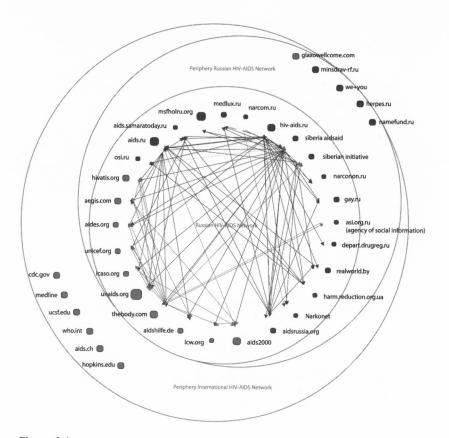

**Figure 3.1**
Russian-language HIV-AIDS Issue Network. Research and graphic by Stephanie
Hankey, Open Society Institute, Budapest, 2001.

Once the entry points to the issue are chosen, the network of organizations dealing with the issue—the issue network—is determined. This
procedure for demarcating the issue network may be performed using
the *Netlocator* or the *IssueCrawler*, (Java) crawler and co-link analysis
applications that crawl the sites of the entry points and capture their outlinks. (The *Netlocator* is depicted in figure 3.2.) Of the outlinks captured,
the analysis engine seeks inter-linkings, returning sets of co-linked sites
in a demarcation procedure. After one or more iterations of the procedure, a network may be found. The degree of co-linking between parties
reveals the extent of the network.[9]

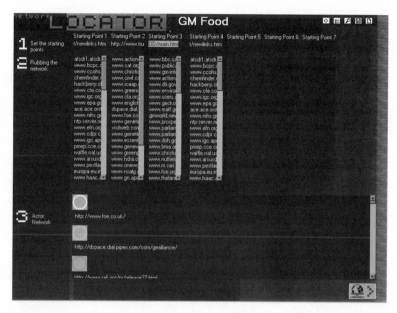

**Figure 3.2**
Rendition of the Netlocator software developed by Govcom.org during the Design & Media Research Fellowship, Jan van Eyck Academy, Maastricht, 1999–2000. Row one shows the starting points. Row two shows the outward links from the starting points, and row three shows the co-links.

With co-link analysis different types of networks may be demarcated. For example, one may desire to find the network exhibiting the highest degree of co-linking or one may wish to find a network with a medium degree of co-linking. The norm of network location we apply is to seek an issue network with an authority (the highest degree of co-linking) that also exhibits *transdiscursivity*. That is, we seek to determine which state of the network is most densely interlinked and is still composed of at least one organization from all of the following domains: .gov, .com, and .org, in the top-level or second-level domains (for example, org.uk is considered an .org for the purposes of analysis). The gov-com-org-domain inclusion parameter shows a state of a debate that includes government, corporations, and civil society. The normativity implied here is that this is the *preferred* debate to be captured and explored.[10] But one may end up locating a gov-com network, a com-org network, or a gov-org network. Each of these network compositions implies different kinds of information societies and/or states of debates, whereby gov-com debates may indicate the settling in of regulatory regimes, and a com-org network an early scandal network around a product exposure case (for example, around Nestlé baby formula or Monsanto's golden rice and terminator gene).[11]

In the exercise in demarcating the food safety issue network, we are interested in knowing whether any issue network may be disclosed from the starting points provided by authoritative newspaper accounts of a debate on food safety. If so, we ask whether the composition of that network reveals debate, and at which intensity and level of territorialization.

Thus, once an issue network is demarcated, it may be queried for properties. The temperature of an issue is gauged by the frequency with which sites dealing with the issue modify their pages. Here "deep pages" are considered; that is, the page modification dates of the portion of the site dealing specifically with the issue, using javascript:alert(document. lastModified). In order to perform such a heat analysis, a few decisions must be made with regard to continuously refreshed sites; for example, the webbified mass media and other sites built atop databases, whereby the pages returned to the browser are generated when they are requested by a browser or a crawler. Here continuous refreshers would not be considered for the metric, and regularly refreshed sites will be considered only when their refreshes depart from their regular schedule. Thus the Issue Barometer, as we dub the display box of the pressure of a social issue within an issue network (located at the base of Issue Network maps), could learn how the sites refresh themselves and then handle refresh histories accordingly. Once the issue barometer has developed that intelligence on the basis of Web dynamics, the refresh histories of organization types can be ascertained, and respective sectoral temperatures (of .govs, .coms, .orgs and various national domains) may be taken. The intensity of the issue engagement (and debate) is measured by the relative quantity of organizations taking positions, through textual analysis.

Finally, the level territorialization of an issue network is gauged by the country composition of the organizations on the map. Here, again, the top-level or second-level domains are of relevance. The query concerns the extent to which the debate party composition (and thus the issue)

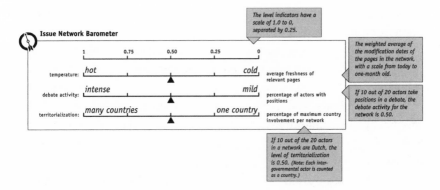

**Figure 3.3**
The Issue Network Barometer with descriptions of the barometric properties.
Graphic by Anderemedia.nl and the Govcom.org Foundation, Amsterdam.

involves one country or many countries, with time series (snapshots of the issue networks over time) revealing whether an issue is de-territorializing or re-territorializing, for example. (See figure 3.3.)

The significance of the level of territorialization (and the rationale behind beginning to chart issue network barometric properties) is exemplified in the case study of HIV-AIDS in Russia (as well as Belarus and Ukraine).[12] In the HIV-AIDS case, basic network location is employed using starting points provided by experts who believe they will disclose a network. Only one iteration of co-link analysis is employed. The entry points and located network actors, as well as the interlinkings between sites, are shown in appendix 3.1. The table results have all the information necessary to make the issue network map in figure 3.1.

The issue network map shows the Russian language network around HIV-AIDS. It indicates regional and international players, differentiated by the grey-scale shadings: the darker shadings are the regional actors and the lighter the international. Node size is an indicator of relative network presence or relevance. The size is relative to the amount of inlinks the site has received from other network actors. The issue network is in the inner circle and the two outer circles show significant peripheral actors of each. The upper right actors are peripheral regional actors, and the lower left are peripheral international actors.

Before a detailed reading of the map, a word should be said about the information design. The circular shape of the issue network visualisation scheme is initially inspired by astronomical charts, and later thought of in terms of a roundtable. The roundtable is meant to express a neo-pluralist potential of the Web, once high on the agenda of the public-spirited Internet writers and developers, viewing the open publishing system of the Internet as a potential challenge to existing hierarchies of credibility and power, as touched on in chapter one. More specifically, the roundtable connotes the neo-pluralist potential of Web-based issue networks and the access of the actors to relevant debate or discussion around the issue. The form and substance of their participation (or their realization of access) is complicated by the known inter-linkings, or entanglements, between actors, shown on the map.

Now I would like to discuss a few of the findings read from the issue network map by the researchers. In studying an issue network for levels of terrorialization, the researchers and I have been interested in the composition of network actors and the entanglements between actors, as well as the question of the sorts of problem definitions taken up by the regional actors on the one hand and the international on the other. The researchers also have been interested in which of these problem definitions and solutions (or "policy considerations") may come to dominate the issue network over time. (As mentioned above, the actor positions are not depicted on this map.)

In the research into HIV-AIDS, we note a disconnection between the international and the regional on both the substantive and the linking levels. For example, of the regional actors, we found a large percentage is drug-related, while the international sites have more to do with sex education. In the Russian-language issue space, HIV-AIDS is seen as an IDU (intravenous drug user) issue, and the international players are generally not recognising the problem as such. Also, the internationals come to the issue network with calls for family support and volunteering, which are part of a more overall strategy of both the UN and the civil society organizations heeding that call. (2001 was the UN's International Year of Volunteers.[13]) Reading the sites, the regionals, however, are not participating in the UN agenda, which might also be called the UN's "calendar work."

The linking between parties is also telling. The regional groups link to the internationals in a particular fashion. Linking from the regional to the international is largely funding-related, reputational or, as we dub it, aspirational; that is, the links made by the regionals to the internationals (most obviously to unaids.org and to osi.ru) are less substantive links pointing to information on the HIV-AIDS situation in the Russian-language area than ones aspiring for recognition. (Osi.ru, for example, has no information on that subject area.) Further reputational linking is on display in the case of the Russian Médecins Sans Frontières Holland site (MSF Holland in Russia). At the time of the network location, the MSF Holland in Russia site was under construction but still received a good number of inlinks from the network. Their reputation precedes them. Significantly, the internationals do not link to the regionals. The Russian groups have not gained a reputation; their substantive input to the problem is also largely ignored, as we found.

Taken together these findings reveal some desperation by the regionals to attract funds, as well as scant substantive grasp on the part of the internationals of the situation closer to the ground in the region. The international issue agendas appear to be too strong. In such a case, we characterise the international's a socio-politically globalizing agenda. Crucially, watching the network and the substance of the network develop over time reveals the extent to which the Russians (as well as the Ukrainian and Byelorussian) assume an agenda driven by global inter-governmental and global civil society issue network actors. By reading the issue network, that particular international community could well begin to rethink whether and when its own aims should come to overshadow those of the regional actors, as the researchers pointed out.

## Mapping the Food Safety Issue in the Netherlands

In order to map any issue one could begin with the question of the identity of its carriers. Who is making an issue out of food safety? To read the newspapers and watch the television news programs, food safety is an issue of some media concern in the Netherlands: Dioxine, BSE, "frankenfoods" (and functional foods), foot and mouth disease, swine fever. Also, the Dutch government has made calls for debate on the issue generally, before authoring new policy documents. More specifically, the government has organized a Publiek Debat on genetically modified foods, with a dedicated website, etenengenen.nl. We begin with the carriers (first, the press) and determine indications of the level of concern and debate. We try to locate the debate by following the media sources; we subsequently track other source sets as the trail heats up. Ultimately, we are especially keen to check whether the debates authored by the press and also by the government bear much relation to debates going on, as it turns out, elsewhere.

Another key question we are asking revolves around the level of indigenousness of the issue; that is, whether the food safety issue has a principal Dutch focus, and which Dutch groups may be the carriers (for example, press, government, non-governmental organizations, consumer groups, alternative movements, producer consortia, and retailers). Or could the issue of food safety be described as an uneasy import from abroad? Perhaps certain Dutch actors are in a Dutch debate only or in an international debate only; perhaps international actors are missing in the Dutch debate (as we found).

Moreover, we are interested in the extent to which the key players, wherever they may be, are engaged in a debate. Is there evidence of a debate underway? By this question of debate, we mean, are key players formulating positions on the issues, and are other key players recognizing and responding to these positions? Are new organizations and groupings forming to join the debate, and are these new groups making efforts to become key players and gain greater presence for their issue definitions, their debate frameworks?

Or should we instead think about the food safety debate as more of a news story? Another way of phrasing the question is as follows: is it possible to find a food safety issue and a food safety debate without relying on a particular form of mediation by the press? In this respect, a basic distinction between a debate and a story of debate may be made. Currently, organizational spokespersons may be responding to journalists' questions about food safety issues, and journalists may be making stories by juxtaposing the spokespersons' viewpoints against each other, and then calling these statement juxtapositions a debate. But here media attention for an issue may mask the absence of debate, or the fact that the debate may be going on elsewhere. Such an absence or displacement of debate may reveal the government and other parties chasing a non-issue, territorially.

In order to answer the question about the extent of debate, one finds a place where organizations air their views on an everyday basis. We continue to propose the Web as a candidate for such a space because it allows for direct broadcasting. Instead of pursuing a disintermediation thesis at this point, we instead would like to characterize organizational airings of positions in terms of "views releases" to issue networks. This is similar to saying that organizations' previous press releases are no longer (only) for the press or public relations, but instead are for networks. Certain organizations may forego press releases all together. They may simply air views whenever a debate heats up, and their views are directed principally to other network actors.

Here we have looked into the Dutch food safety debate through the lens of the Web, in the above sense of reading views releases. We queried key players' Web sites directly. As discussed above, we have created means to measure the pulse of an issue in these spaces. How frequently are the key players in the network uploading ("releasing") their views? The frequency with which the issue pages on a sample of organizations' Web sites are modified is taken as a measure of the heat of the debate, in terms of airings. We also are interested in whether the organizations are taking positions in the debate and whether these positions are directed at other actors in the Netherlands, or perhaps at international actors. This will aid us in locating the debate substantively.

In the following, we explain the means by which the key players involved in various Dutch food safety issues are located, and how the composition of the key parties (who's in, who's out?) also may be interpreted. By noting position-taking activity as well as the organizations' country origins, we are able to provide indications of the debate intensity and de-territorialization and depict them, below the maps, in the discursive and Issue Barometer rectangular boxes.

### Where is the Dutch Food Safety Debate?

At the outset, we will trust the press and its characterization of food safety as a debate taking place in the Netherlands. In fact, we desire to harden the press claim, if possible, and learn who is active and what the debate is about so we can put the debate (and some indicators of it) on display. From news stories in the *Algemeen Dagblad* and the AVRO TV station a number of initial Dutch parties to a food safety debate are identified.[14] These are the names of the organizations mentioned in the

**Table 3.3**
Food Safety Issue Network 1: List of Parties to Media-only Debate.

http://www.gezondsite.nl

http://www.voedsel.net

http://www.biotechnologie.pagina.nl

http://www.pz.nl/akb

http://www.greenpeace.nl

http://www.voedselveiligheid.nl

http://www.minvrom.nl/milieu/ggo

http://www.voedingscentrum.org

http://www.voeding.tno.nl

http://info.omroep.nl/ncrv

newspaper and on the TV Web site about the debate—the journalists' sources and/or recommendations. Running these sites through one iteration of the network location software (for we trust the experts, as in the Russian example above), it is telling to find that these sites as a group are held together by one party—one that links copiously and receives many links. The one common networked site is http://info.omroep.nl/avro, the Dutch TV broadcasting company. This suggests that these sites are held together by a current affairs TV program on food safety; some of the organizations in this group were mentioned in the program, and they, proudly, link to it. The TV show becomes the only glue (or common link) binding these organizations. (See table 3.3.)

The debate, if we could even call it that, is a mediated juxtaposition of talking heads, with statements as well as b-roll (the term used in the industry for background footage put on screen to enliven and overlay the talk), with organizations subsequently linking to the show to say, proudly, that they have been on TV.

Returning to the network, one notes that the sites are all Dutch. While individual sites in the network do link to international sites, no two Dutch sites link to the same international site. Thus the knowledge of relevant international sites (one link interpretation) is not shared across the network. We report a territorialized media issue only.

On the Dutch AVRO page dedicated to the program, there is one international player—foodnews.org. When one adds www.foodnews.org to the list of starting points and performs a series of iterations of technique, the network gradually internationalizes, drifting away from the Netherlands; the issue also begins to heat up and become more intense with .org's responding directly to .com's.

We decide, initially, not to follow that promising network thread abroad, but instead look deeper into the Dutch debate space. Perhaps the broadcasting company and the newspaper did not exert themselves in the search for parties to a debate, either by seeking networks or by finding less mediated exchanges through source recommendations made by search engines, list contributions, or similar sources. They have other methods for locating and staging debate. Instead, we decide to locate and map sub-networks, with starting points provided by comprehensive link lists on single sites dedicated to particular aspects of food and food safety. The point here is to ascertain the extent to which there may be mini-debates in sub-networks awaiting some further glue to bind them together—an incident, an announcement of a public debate, or a White Paper. We look into a kind of "real food" movement, which we believe may lead us to a debate.

Up until now we have found only a modicum of debate, defined in terms of views releases, reactions, and (re)positionings. In the sub-space, we note little in the way of Web dialogue or linkage outside of a small Dutch food movement. Theirs is a network of actors engaged in organic production—delivery as well as labelling. The substance attributed to the small network is gleaned from the recurrence of key words; that is, labels (*keurmerken*) being the most common, telling term shared by a majority of the sites in the network. Some of the makings of debate lie in the Alternative Consumers' Union's long, critical report on all the labels, but the other parties did not respond in kind with positions and standpoints.[15] They allow the opportunity for debate to pass. In all, we note that the sites in the network are primarily providing (not very fresh) information about the groups' causes, information on how product is produced, where to order and buy, how to sign up for a tour of a farm, when and where to take an eco-holiday, how to subscribe to the magazine, and how to donate. These are lifestyle movement networks, held together substantively by labelling, with a sole critical party attempting to open a debate. (See table 3.4 and figure 3.4.)

**Table 3.4**
Food Safety Issue Network 2: List of Parties in the "Biologisch" Food
Movement Network.

http://www.skal.com

http://www.platformbiologica.nl

http://www.ecomarkt.nl

http://www.dekleineaarde.nl

http://www.jonasmagazine.nl

http://www.pz.nl/akb (alternatieve konsumentenbond)

http://www.denatuurwinkel.nl

http://www.ekodirect.com

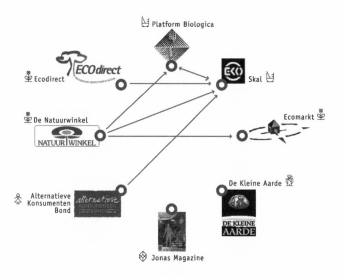

Dutch Organic Food Lifestyle Network, July 2001

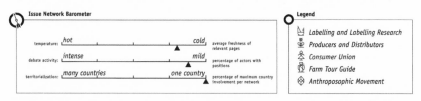

**Figure 3.4**
Dutch Organic Food Lifestyle Network, 2001, with issue barometric properties.
Graphic by Anderemedia.nl and the Govcom.org Foundation, Amsterdam.

**Table 3.5**
List of Actors in Dutch Food Safety Debate, according to the *NRC Handelsblad*.

http://www.voedingscentrum.org/stud0005.html

http://bse.pagina.nl

http://www.minlnv.nl/infomart/extern.htm

http://www.voedselveiligheid.nl/bin/toon_sub.php3?sub_rubriek='72'

http://www.keuringsdienstvanwaren.nl/snelweg/links.html

http://www.pz.nl/akb/links/linkadressen.html

http://www.minvws.nl

http://www.consumentenbond.nl/asp/onderwerp/gezond.asp?node_id=4455&
version_id=1

*Source*: *NRC Handelsblad* Dossier, July 17, 2001, http://www.nrc.nl/dossiers.

In our continuing quest for the Dutch debate through network location and eventually multiple and interconnected views releases, we turn to a bedrock establishment newspaper, the *NRC Handelsblad*, and the file (*dossier*) on the food safety debate found on its site. (See table 3.5.) To bring into perspective the selection of an established newspaper as source of new starting points for network and debate location, it is important to point out that the creation of the *NRC Handelblad*'s debate file site, on February 15, 2001, comes at a time when the government is formulating its new policy document, or White Paper, on food safety, eventually delivered to Parliament on July 18, 2001.[16] Thus, apart from the TV news program and the other media outlets touched on above, the *NRC Handelsblad* may be thought of as both a source and a resource, among many, for staffers and others researching the state of the debate and eventually addressing some of the debate points in the policy document. We assume the staffers will not concern themselves with small food movements, though the movement's issue of labelling is our only clue of where a debate may be found. (We also confirm this impression of labelling, forming some substance of the debate, in a short, vertical storyline analysis of the government White Paper, in table 3.6.[17])

Labelling is mentioned as one of the governmental policy instruments for food safety, next to norms and bans; the norms and labels come from the Codex Alimentarius Commission and from the EU, we learn. (The WTO is also deemed a key player.)

**Table 3.6**
Government Food Safety White Paper: Vertical Key Word Storyline Analysis.

BSE-crisis
Dioxine
DON
Voedselinfecties; incidenten keten,
buitenland-binnenland complex

Toegenomen informatie
Perceptie van de consument
Communicatie
Consumentenbescherming

Internationale afspraken
Normen, Codex Alimentarius, G8, European Union
Risicoanalyse (wetenschappelijke beoordeling; beheer;
communicatie)

Dioxine publiciteitscrisis (Berenschot)

Meer kennis—Internet
Overheid bijdrage: sites, krantenadvertenties
Voorstel: Barcodescanners (vrijwillig / winkels)
ICT en ketensystemen (Chaperonneprogramma)

Aanpakken bij de bron (primaire verantwoordelijkheid
bedrijfsleven)
Risicobeoordeling (relatie: maximale inname stof / levensduur
bevolking)
Hazard Analysis (HAACP)
Normstelling (Handhaafbaarheid technisch / financieel)

Overheidsinstrumenten—Etikettering, Consumptieadviezen,
Verbieden
Doel—Doorlichting bedrijfsprocessen

Normstelling (maar WTO)
Codex Alimentarius
Nederlandse instrumenten (voedsel consumptiepeiling)
EU Witboek Voedselveiligheid
Ook Nederlandse Wetgeving (Warenwet o.a.)
Onvoldoende voor crisismaatregelen (behalve Destructiewet o.a.)

Spoedmaatregelen nodig
Doorlichting Integrale ketensystemen
Early warning

In oprichting: Nederlandse Voedselautoriteit (NVa)
Traceerbaarheid; opsporing
Communicatie in crisissituaties
Vertrouwen van overheid en consument

*Source*: Ministerie van Landbouw, Natuurbeheer en Visserij, and Ministerie van Volksgezondheid, Welzijn en Sport, 2001. Author's notes.

The state of the issue network (and perhaps the debate) are checked on July 17 and 18, around the time of the delivery of the White Paper to Parliament. The *NRC Handelsblad*, in its dossier still unchanged from February, points to actors that have certain outgoing links in common. In the list of pointers are the government, government-sponsored NGOs, consumer groups, and newly created food safety and food portals with link lists and, occasionally, news. (Appendixes 3.2 and 3.3 list the actors and the interlinking among them.)

The issue network in figure 3.5 has certain dynamics similar to our organic food network—a set of interlinked, mainly information sites, with scant substantive positionings apart from those at the Consumer Union, at the Codex Alimentarius Commission, and at a Dutch Ministry (Agriculture). Under labelling, the Consumer Union has the position that claims to the nutritional value of functional foods (which could be a criterion behind a label) require previous empirical demonstration. The Codex Alimentarius Commission positions itself in favour of some form of labelling (albeit with the presence of allergens, not nutritional value, behind the label). Finally, the Dutch Ministry comes forward with the standpoint that there should be a debate. All other parties are mute on the debate—whether there is one, should be one, or indeed could be one.

Where the properties of the network are concerned, the relevant pages taken as a whole are only marginally fresher than the organic network's. With positions being taken by very few actors and stale page modification behaviour, we can contextualize the debate-seeking position taken by the Ministry. (There is no debate!) Where territorialization is concerned, the network now includes a few international actors (US and EU governmental sites as well as the FAO/WHO Codex Alimentarius Commission), with links running to that higher-level labelling debate taking place at Codex as well as at the EU. The Codex Commission, as we mentioned, has put allergen labelling on the table in one of its policy framings of the food safety issue. The EU, we note in their network page, will be considering those labelling proposals. (We consider these clues as promising for eventually locating a debate.)

The Dutch Government White Paper, put forward by two Ministries (one of which is in the network) reads unequivocally, however, that Dutch policy will follow the Codex Alimentarius Commission's and the EU's recommendations on norms as well as labelling (unless they break

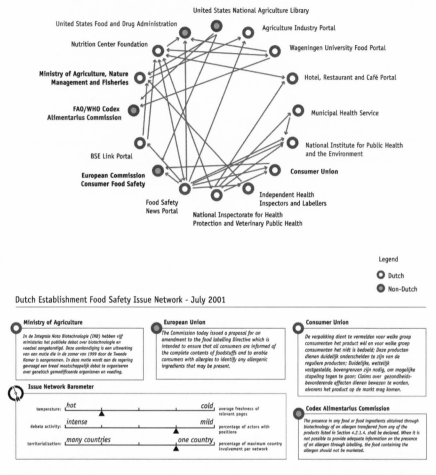

**Figure 3.5**
The Dutch Establishment Food Safety Issue Network, 2001, with issue barometric properties and positions taken in the debate. Graphic by Anderemedia.nl and the Govcom.org Foundation, Amsterdam.

Dutch law). For its position to matter, the Consumer Union, it appears, will have to put its views before the EU and the Codex Alimentarius. (The Consumer Union does show knowledge of the relevance of the EU by linking to it.)

Put differently, by reading the properties of the issue network (and one deeper-linked White Paper document), one could conclude that the Dutch debate is not taking place in the Netherlands, but rather at the Codex Alimentarius Commission and the EU. Let us first attempt to bring it back to the Netherlands, with the government-organized public debate on genetically modified food, before leaving the buildings again.

## The Dutch Food Safety Debate Leaves the Netherlands

The public debate organized by the Dutch government on genetically modified food in 2001 falls in a long territorial tradition, from the broad social discussion on energy (and the *sociale kaarten*) of the 1980s through those in the 1990s and early 2000s on a variety of concerns as mobility, genetic screening, cloning, and xeno-transplantation. The debates also fit into a broader international movement, where models and specific formats and programming techniques are presented at international conferences.[18] The various national bodies—for example, Rathenau in the Netherlands—have their own names and variations on these debates and often export them (or watch them move) to other countries: consensus conferences (from Denmark to the UK, Canada, U.S., and beyond), citizen juries (U.S. to Australia), and so on.[19] In the Dutch public debate formula (a variation of which is exported by a Dutch agency, HIVOS, to developing countries[20]), citizens are called upon in newspaper ads and, ultimately, weekend retreats, to formulate issue problematizations and positions. These new policy proposals are discussed with established social groups and stakeholders in further sessions, and eventually the outcomes are presented in high-profile forums with experts and "opinion-makers" on hand to vet their feasibility and create momentum. The entire process is part of a Dutch tradition, the Polder Model, which has its origins in wage negotiations between employer groups and unions in 1982.

There are two outcomes of the 2001 public debate on genetically modified food from the final report that are worthy of mention in relation to

**Figure 3.6**
The logos of the 15 Dutch NGOs that left the government-organized public debate on GM Food in 2001. Source: http://www.gentechdebat.nl/conferentie, captured on October 19, 2001.

the issue network findings.[21] The first is one of the report's overall conclusions, gathered from surveys and (low) debate Web site visitorship as reported by the head of the commission in the press.[22] Contrary to Denmark, Germany, and the UK, the Dutch public is not interested in the issue, or in the debate. (Perhaps more damningly to the small amount of Dutch debate we found, the Commissioner also said the Dutch do not even read the product labels in the supermarket.[23]) Secondly, it was learned that fifteen Dutch NGOs decided, mid-way, to no longer to take part in the proceedings, citing mistrust in the debate, pre-set outcomes, and thus the overall legitimacy of classic politics. Indeed, the organizations, as is customary in civil society, set up their own counter-debate in rapid time, at gentechdebat.nl and in a building.[24]

Taking these 15 organizations as the starting points for the location of a debate leads to a complicated global issue network, where certain of the actors in the Dutch establishment food safety debate are present, albeit with far less relevance than those that left the Dutch debate. (As one would expect, perhaps, the counter-debate, gentechdebat.nl, has greater presence in the issue network than the government debate, etenengenen.nl. See also figure 3.6.) Indeed, we have finally found a rich and rather tightly interlinked issue network, where terms of debate are shared and exchanges made. These terms and exchanges are on a higher level of abstraction than those in the Netherlands—than those in the organic food network, in the *NRC Handelsblad*'s establishment network, in the public debate report, or in the White Paper (apart from a set of brackets in that report). Rather than norms and labelling as the issue, leading, ultimately, to the Codex Alimentarius Commission and the EU, much of the debate revolves around alternatives to "patents on life," where certain products (such as golden rice) and reactions by far-flung farmers become the glue that holds together the substance of the network. The debate moves from Codex to the WTO, a parenthetically mentioned institution in the government's White Paper. Where the issue network's properties are concerned, it is far hotter and de-territorialized; southern participation is greater.

## The Challenges of De-territorialization and Re-territorialization

A series of possible conclusions can be drawn from these observations, apart from the obvious fact that issue network analysis on the Web often leads researchers to global debates led by civil society and inter-governmental organizations, with certain multinational products mentioned across sites. We could attempt to disarm the issue network approach on the grounds that the Web leads one precisely in this globalising direction, if it were not for the fact that conclusions about de-territorialization of issues, debates, policies, and laws are repeatedly reported in the international and national public debate and politics literature by academic and governmental researchers. Thus we confirm a previous impression rather than make an astounding claim. But here, from the findings, we wish to make a case more normatively against the repeated improvement of techniques that ensure better territorial citizen debate, by refining forums and debate spaces on and off the Web.[25] (Alongside de-territorialization, refinement of public debate techniques is another outcome in the national literature and in practice.) To make such a case we would like to drop the citizen debate construct and instead contribute the issue network as the political debate space. But, mainly, we would like to re-interpret how to read the poor outcomes of the territorialized food safety debate, returning to one of the original questions: where is the Dutch food safety debate, who is in it, and what is it about?

From the territorial citizen debate point of view (and its management by government), many of the observations are depressing—lack of societal debate, public disinterest in government-organized debate, public weariness of social issues, and eyes glossing over meticulously codified product labels at supermarkets. Let us rewrite these outcomes—first, very briefly, along the lines in some of the other established argumentation on public understanding—and finally in terms of the arguments made from a new understanding of the challenges of re-territorialization. Once a public is brought to life through surveys and organized citizen debate, public disinterest in genetically modified food may be read, just as conventionally, as an understanding by the public that there is not a Dutch debate, nor would one matter. Here one attributes intelligence to publics, which is a common move in the literature.[26] Similarly, social group disinterest, often understood as mistrust in the process as well as in pre-set outcomes, may have an additional reading that is not normative but methodological. The departure of the 15 social groups is a clear indication that they have an understanding of where a debate is located. They are not so much leaving it as they are leading one to it.[27] Apart from their capacity to lead us to an issue network and debate, another sure sign that they are part of the debate is their ability to re-stage it on short notice (and have it resonate globally), as was the case with gentechdebat.nl within the global issue network.

Following these observations, one could argue that attempts by governmental commissions (and government Web sites) to relocate the debate should be viewed and evaluated in terms of their capacity to retain the parties already in the debate. Attempts to move debate may be read along the lines of their ability to capture the existing terms of it, and indeed keep the parties already in the debate interested in its newly territorialized progression. After all, with de-territorialization the norm, re-territorialization (by government or others) should be seen as a counter-movement in search of legitimacy. In any event, both the much discussed norm of public disinterest and the far more significant migration of the social groups back to the vibrant debate space point to the crisis of national public debate. Thus, one may argue as we have done for capturing existing social debate networks (amongst social groups, governments, corporations, media, and even citizens, if present) rather than authoring the disappointment of an ideal.

Finally, once the issue and the debate are located, the Dutch situation on the ground becomes clearer and far less depressing. Recall in the organic food sub-network the lament about the Alternative Consumer's Union; no party took up its invitation to debate labelling. But the union has a presence in the global network; its contribution, however small, lies not in the sub-network of the Dutch real food movement, but in one much greater. Thus we need not worry ourselves about the other Dutch organic parties passing on the opportunity to respond in kind and position themselves in a debate on labels. Indeed, the other farmers, distributors and labellers, absent from the global debate, are understandably more concerned with the good life nationally. We shall leave them to it. We propose no longer inviting them to issue forums. Rather, we shall meet them at market.

## Appendixes

### Appendix 3.1   Network Location Method and Data: Russian-language HIV-AIDs Issue Network

Starting points

1. http://www.hiv-aids.ru
2. http://public.tsu.ru:8080/~aidsaid
3. http://www.aids.ru

The actors below have been located through one iteration of co-link analysis from the starting points. The listing shows the inter-linking between organizations in the core network. The organizations in the periphery on the map received at least two links from the core network actors. Those links are not depicted on the map, and are not listed below.

— "( )" are "links from" the starting points 1, 2 and/or 3.
— Under the URL are "links to" the network.

osi.ru
http://www.osi.ru (1,2)
no links to the network

aids.ru
http://www.aids.ru (1,2)
links to: aids2000.com, aegis.com, unaids.org, aids.samaratoday.ru, namesfund.ru, thebody.com, hivatis.org, icaso.org, aides.org, aidshilfe.de

aids.samaratoday.ru
http://www.aids.samaratoday.ru (1,3)
links to: unaids.org, unicef.org

msfholru.org
http://www.msfholru.org (1,2,3)
site under construction—no links

medlux.ru
http://www.medlux.ru (1,2,3)
no links to the network

narcom.ru
http://www.narcom.ru (1,2)
links to: postman.ru/~narkonet/

hiv-aids.ru
http://www.hiv-aids.ru (2,3)
links to: osi.ru, aids.ru, msfholru.org, medlux.ru, narcom.ru, alien.ru/
~sibin, aidsrussia.org, narconon.ru, gay.ru, public.tsu.ru:8080/~aidsaid,
aids.samaratoday.ru, depart.drugreg.ru, realworld.unibel.by, medlux.ru,
harm.reduction.org.ua/aaf

siberia aidsaid
http://public.tsu.ru:8080/~aidsaid (1,2,3)
links to: aegis.com, thebody.com, hivatis.org, unaids.org, icw.org,
aides.org, aidshilfe.de, aids2000.com, aids.ru, hiv-aids.ru, medlux.ru,
gay.ru, msfholru.org, aidsrussia.org, alien.ru/~sibin, narconon.ru, aids.ru

siberian initiative
http://www.alien.ru/~sibin (1,2,3)
links to: medlux.ru, msfholru.org, aidsrussia.org, realworld.unibel.by,
postman.ru/~narkonet, aids.ru

narconon.ru
http://www.narconon.ru (1,2)
no links to the network

gay.ru
http://www.gay.ru (1,2,3)
no links to the network

asi.org.ru (agency of social information)
http://www.asi.org.ru (2,3)
links to: thebody.com

depart.drugreg.ru
http://www.depart.drugreg.ru (1,3)
no links to the network

realworld.by
http://www.realworld.unibel.by (1,3)
links to: aids.ru

harm.reduction.org.ua
http://harm.reduction.org.ua/aaf (1,3)
links to: aids.ru

narkonet
http://www.postman.ru/~narkonet (narkonet) (2,3)
no links to the network

aidsrussia.org
http://aidsrussia.org (1,2)
links to: public.tsu.ru:8080/~aidsaid, aids.ru, realworld.unibel.by,
gay.ru, alien.ru/~sibin, msfholru.org, hiv-aids.ru, medlux.ru

aids2000
http://www.aids2000.com (2,3)
site is down—no links

icw.org
http://www.icw.org (2,3)
links to: aids2000.com

aidshilfe.de
http://www.aidshilfe.de (2,3)
links to: aegis.com

thebody.com
http://www.thebody.com (2,3)
links to: unaids.org, icaso.org, icw.org, aides.org, aidshilfe.de,
hivatis.org, aegis.com, public.tsu.ru:8080/~aidsaid, alien.ru/~sibin,
unicef.org, asi.org.ru

unaids.org
http://www.unaids.org (2,3)
link to: unicef.org

icaso.org
http://www.icaso.org (2,3)
links to: unaids.org, aids2000.com

unicef.org
http://www.unicef.org (2,3)
links to: unaids.org

aides.org
http://www.aides.org (2,3)
links to: unaids.org

aegis.com
http://www.aegis.com (2,3)
links to: thebody.com, aids2000.com, hivatis.org

hivatis.org
http://www.hivatis.org (2,3)
links to: thebody.com, unaids.org

**Appendix 3.2    Actors in the Dutch Establishment Food Safety Issue Network, 2001**

| | |
|---|---|
| United States National Agriculture Library | http://www.nal.usda.gov/ref/govern.htm |
| Agriculture Industry Portal | http://www.agriwide.nl |
| Wageningen University Food Portal | http://www.voedsel.net |
| Hotel, Restaurant and Café Portal | http://www.bedr-horeca.nl |
| Municipal Health Service | http://www.ggd.nl |
| National Institute for Public Health and the Environment | http://www.rivm.nl |
| Consumer Union | http://www.consumentenbond.nl |
| Independent Health Inspectors and Labellers | http://www.skal.com |
| National Inspectorate for Health Protection and Veterinary Public Health | http://www.keuringsdienstvanwaren.nl |
| Food Safety News Portal | http://www.voedselveiligheid.nl |
| European Commission Consumer Food Safety | http://europa.eu.int/comm/dgs/health_consumer/index_nl.htm and http://europa.eu.int/comm/food/index_nl.html |

| BSE Portal | http://bse.pagina.nl |
| FAO/WHO Codex Alimentarius Commission | http://www.fao.org/waicent/faoinfo/esn/codex/default.htm |
| Ministry of Agriculture, Nature Management, and Fisheries | http://www.minlnv.nl |
| Nutrition Center Foundation | http://www.voedingscentrum.org |
| United States Food and Drug Administration | http://www.fda.gov |

**Appendix 3.3  Interlinking among Actors in the Dutch Establishment Food Safety Issue Network, 2001**

United States National Agriculture Library
http://www.nal.usda.gov/ref/govern.htm
links to: minlnv.nl, fao.org, europa.eu.int

Agriculture Industry Portal
http://www.agriwide.nl
no links to network

Wageningen University Food Portal
http://www.voedsel.net
links to: voedingscentrum.org, fao.org, fda.gov

Hotel, Restaurant and Café Portal
http://www.bedr-horeca.nl
links to: voedingscentrum.org

Municipal Health Service
http://www.ggd.nl
links to: rivm.nl

National Institute for Public Health and Environment
http://www.rivm.nl
no links to the network

Consumer Union
http://www.consumentenbond.nl
links to: europa.eu.int

Independent Health Inspectors and Labellers
http://www.skal.com
links to: minlnv.nl

National Inspectorate for Health Protection and Veterinary Public Health
http://www.keuringsdienstvanwaren.nl
links to: consumentenbond.nl, rivm.nl, ggd.nl, voedingscentrum.nl, bedr-horeca.nl

Food Safety News Portal
http://www.voedselveiligheid.nl
links to: bse.pagina.nl, rivm.nl, europa.eu.int, voedingscentrum.org, fda.gov, agriwide.nl, consumentenbond.nl, skal.com

European Commission Consumer Food Safety
http://europa.eu.int/comm/dgs/health_consumer/index_nl.htm          and
http://europa.eu.int/comm/food/index_nl.html
no links to the network

BSE Link Portal
http://bse.pagina.nl
links to: minlnv.nl, voedingscentrum.nl, voedselveiligheid.nl

FAO/WHO Codex Alimentarius Commission
http://www.fao.org/waicent/faoinfo/esn/codex/default.htm
no links to the network

Ministry of Agriculture, Nature Management and Fisheries
http://www.minlnv.nl
links to: agriwide.nl

Nutrition Center Foundation
http://www.voedingscentrum.nl
links to:    www.keuringsdienstvanwaren.nl,    www.bedr-horeca.nl, voedselveiligheid.nl, fda.gov, voedsel.net

United States Food and Drug Administration
http://www.fda.gov
no links to the network

The Codex Alimentarius Commission has moved to http://www.codexalimentarius.net.

# 4

## After Genoa: Remedying Informational Politics and Augmenting Reality with the Web

### Introduction

In the previous chapter we have argued that the debates of substance are often not the ones authored by the press, or by the government. Juxtaposed statements in the press or the convening of disinterested citizen parties and other non-debating social groups also may not be the means of generating a debate, especially when the terms of a debate that interest the few engaged parties (our Alternative Consumer Union as well as the Consumer Union) are being formulated elsewhere (Codex Alimentarius Commission, the EU, and the WTO). The more telling debate space may be found, eventually, by following the actors who appear to know where this elsewhere is located—the 15 Dutch NGOs. Working with this debate-tracing heuristic, we propose a new form of issue maps, contextualized in the Dutch tradition of *sociale kaarten*—the issue network maps. Apart from putting the issue actors and the emerging debate on display, the maps provide new readings and indicators of issues; that is, interpretations of aspirations, reputations, and knowledge by reading between the links; the display of positions as well as missing positions; and, finally, the issue barometric properties indicating measures of heat, activity, and territorialization. The manner in which one utilizes the maps depends on the questions one is posing. Of interest to us were the questions, where is the Dutch food safety debate, and what is it about? Is the government capturing the debate in its policy documents and in its organized public debates? If not, what could it be reading and putting on display in order to capture the debate and also show where it stands in relation to other debating parties? We have proposed a heuristic—follow the parties already in the debate, capture the debate, then show it. The heuristic and the findings have led to some further considerations, too. If a debate is to be relocated territorially and organized in buildings or on Web sites, are the terms of the debate of interest to the parties already in it? Answering this question goes hand and hand with the question of the credibility and legitimacy of a government-organized debate. Is it social or merely governmental? When would the organization of a public debate not matter? How could one tell in advance?

In the process of asking and identifying where the action is and leading the debate-seeker to issue networks, often (but not always) made up of civil society actors and inter-governmental organizations, we have been asked about the familiarity of the civil society agendas. Certain inquisitors have questioned whether or not civil society aims are already largely known, perhaps because they are adequately covered in the press and other familiar printed and Web matter. The aims, some inquisitors have thought, would be covered—especially around events when certain civil society groups attempt to make their presence and their issues felt—at major summits. This chapter pursues that question, answers it negatively, and ultimately makes a case for an instrument that captures and streams (some) civil society issues. The method we follow is different from the previous instruments, for we do not know in advance what the issues and the specifics are; we only know that there are issues—important ones about globalization—that bring thousands to the streets where summit participants meet.

Returning to our inquisitor's questions for a moment, when one immerses oneself in matters of the adequacies of issue representation and coverage, one enters a highly contested area. We shall tread that area carefully and attempt to address some of the larger positions taken about whether and when issues are adequately represented. In order to do so, we first present the foundations of this instrument that captures and streams civil society aims, which eventually can be employed *in situ* at summits. (Our instrument regularly queries the issues that a definitive list of the Seattle actors as well as a Dutch group of NGOs are campaigning for. Having one national and one international group, for comparison sake, is in concert with the concerns of the previous chapter on overlaps and differences between territorial and de-territorial concerns, though we do not pursue that question again here.) Thereafter we shall attempt to defend the principle behind the instrument in discussing the adequacy of coverage of the issues put forward by civil society counter-summiteers at the G8 summit in Genoa. We must defend the dedicated civil society stream in terms of the sorts of arguments made not only by our inquisitor above (who may think that we already know civil society issues and aims through the press), but also those made by highly critical press analysts (who, in line with analysts of informational politics, argue that we may never know). Thus we shall be arguing on two levels, empirically (are the civil society aims covered?) and analytically (can we confirm certain analysts' understandings of what is covered, what is not, and why?).

### The Web Issue Index: Aggregating Global Civil Society and Demystifying Protesters

The Web Issue Index is prototypical tracking instrumentation providing regular indications of leading (global and national) social issues, according to the Web. The Web Issue Index strives to harness the forecasting value of "word on net," and distill issue trends for multiple issue analytical work.

The Web Issue Index is comprised of two telling baskets of "issue-making sources[1]." Both baskets (listed in appendixes 4.1 and 4.2) comprise civil society organizations (CSOs), a Dutch national set and an international set, albeit with a U.S. international frame.[2] The first, the Echte Welvaart (or "genuine welfare") basket, is made up of those Dutch civil society groups of various stripes that joined the Echte Welvaart campaign.[3] The second is an international group of campaigning organizations on the streets of Seattle during the WTO meeting in 1999, and all mentioned in the eyewitness book, *Five Days that Shook the World: Seattle and Beyond*.[4] The baskets of issue-making sources on the Web are queried for issue lists on a regular basis.[5] The Seattle basket is the most active, and is queried monthly for issues. Somewhat more stable in their issue selection and campaigning, the Dutch Echte Welvaart basket is queried bi-monthly. (We return to the refresh rates below.)

The issues listed on each of the sites of the basket actors are sought, and co-issue occurrence analysis is performed. The purpose of seeking issue co-occurrence relates to deriving the issues of collective significance. The recurring issues are placed in the index, and then compared to the previous periods; a month ago for the Seattle basket, and two months ago for the Echte Welvaart basket. With this comparative data, the Web Issue Index shows the rise (and fall) of issues over time.

The main body of the chapter makes an argument about the significance and distinctiveness of the source pools for issue identification, in comparison both to other issue-makers on the Web (UN, World Bank, Oneworld) as well as to more conventional issue-makers, the press. There is also a discussion of the suitability of the Web more generally for issue awareness, in a follow-up to the discussion in the previous chapter about the challenges of understanding issues without the Web.

One may inquire into the relevance and rigor of using the particular source baskets as well as the Web more generally for deriving the issue indexes as described above. Where the first inquiry is concerned—the relevance and rigor of basket selection—a number of explanations are in order. The first relates to the notion of a telling set of sources comprising the baskets. Why would the Seattle protesters be a telling list of actors from whence to derive lists of social issues? The selection of actors that make up the Seattle Index—from the eyewitness book—relies on a watershed and highly symbolic event that arguably made global civil society into an aggregated social actor set. (See also figure 4.1.) Given the historical context, understanding the place and positions of a new actor set brought to life in Seattle as an object of issue research, a news-maker as well as an agent of social change, is one rationale behind building an index of this nature.[6] But, equally, there is an opportunity to demystify Seattle—perhaps allow it to speak on its own terms or at least on the terms that may be derived from embedded information and Web dynamics, as opposed to those of the press. Shortly, we return to the empirical question of the distinctiveness of the issues put forward by the issue-makers on the Web (and the streets) by contrasting the issue lists in print newspapers and on activist and official Web sites around the Genoa G8 summit.

Secondly, there's the concern of using a basket of CSO sources. Analytically, one could argue that such basket-making collectivizes, or in the new terminology, aggregates, voices. Indeed, making source baskets in our manner fits with the picture emerging around the transformation of issue politics (as alluded to in chapter three). Once understood in terms of single-issue groups (or special interest groups),[7] global civil society is

**Figure 4.1**
Rock Star Games has come out with State of Emergency, a video game where you can play an activist as on the streets of Seattle during the WTO meetings in 1999. It's of the "urban riot" genre and has proved popular enough to merit a sequel. One of the elements noticeably absent on the screens is information and communications technology, such as a walkie-talkie, a mobile telephone, a PDA, and a hand-held or laptop computer with wireless connectivity. Source: http://www.gamespot.co.uk/stories/screens/0,2160,2087213–4,00.html, accessed on June 13, 2001.

being aggregated and viewed as a *multiple issue* player. Examples of global civil society issue aggregators are NGO and issue news-makers such as Oneworld International.[8] Dedicated to global justice, Oneworld has upwards of 1,000 partner NGOs whose sites are crawled regularly for fresh stories and put on the Oneworld.net site in the style of BBC news online. Of special interest, too, is Indymedia, with sister organizations (franchises) set up in a number of countries, publishing stories from alternative, freelance journalists, often on the ground and in the communications centers at major summit protest events. Both sites attract millions of hits, though Indymedia does not keep its log files for security reasons.[9] Once one takes on board the idea that there are multiple-issue collectives, means may be developed to chart issue movements according to similar aggregated groupings.

It should be pointed out that the Web Issue Index takes a different approach to the above aggregators in a number of respects. It does not amalgamate *news* by a variety of partner NGOs or solidarity journalists, as in the Oneworld and the Indymedia cases, respectively. We also are not endeavoring to make news per se, or to attract a campaigning organization or similar group to tailor their communications to our format, as news organizations do. (One of the claims to fame of the critical art group, RTmark.com, has been their ability to manufacture newsworthy stories in the form of a short videobites—cans easily digestible for broadcasters. They post videotapes of their stories to broadcasters, and have had some success in penetrating the commercial news.) Critical art groups aside, NGOs and movement actors often purposely strive for media coverage, a subject discussed later (here and in chapter five). Moreover, the organizations are unaffiliated to the issue indexing project. In the Web Issue Index the organizations are not knowingly participating in the aggregation, and the baskets are not open to interested parties to join, as is the usual, inclusive culture of the movement. Thus there is some critical distance between the aggregator and the aggregated, between indexing project and the movement. The Web Issue Index, in other words, is not voluntaristic, a subject discussed in chapter one.

Instead, we take advantage of a largely *given* information delivery style of our collective(s)—the issue list. We make the Index by stablizing groupings—the Echte Welvaart set and the Seattle set—and then we watch how stable sets of actors define their issues over time. Additionally, we may ascertain the lengths of time particular issues are of currency to these sets, eventually noting attention spans in comparison with governmental as well as press attention spans, as we do in the following chapter.

Allow us briefly to situate the notion of our collective, of (global) civil society as an issue-maker, in competition with other issue-makers first on the Web, and later off the Web.[10] To gain a sense of the space in which an issue aggregator such as Oneworld International is operating, it is instructive to compare its issue list with those on the issue portals of the World Bank (the e-Development Gateway)[11] and the United Nations. The point is to demonstrate issue list competition between parties and the normality of issue lists (and thus the suitability of them for analysis), as well as the distinctiveness of one global civil society listing. The issue list is a format shared by NGOs, IFIs and IGOs. Figures 4.2, 4.3 and 4.4 are the issue portals of Oneworld, the World Bank, and the UN, respectively. Note in table 4.1 that only five topics or issues overlap across the three issue portals.

**Figure 4.2**
Oneworld International's topics, captured on August 16, 2001.

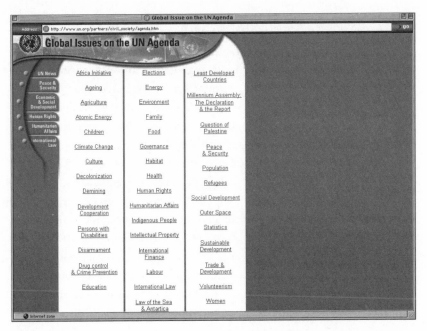

**Figure 4.3**
Issues on the United Nations agenda, captured on August 16, 2001.

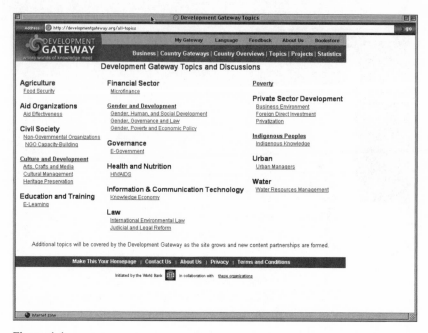

**Figure 4.4**
World Bank's Development Gateway Topics and Discussions, captured on August 16, 2001.

So far we have argued that on the Web a collective grouping of newly significant issue-makers may be tracked for issue movements in an approach differing from other issue aggregators and other (press) monitoring practices. In the brief comparison, it is noted that the issue-makers representing or even comprising a notional global civil society have sets of issues fairly distinct from their issue list competitors at the World Bank and the UN. In speaking about competition, we also could take note of the similar styles of issue presentation on portal-type pages with their own stories and projects behind them. Significantly, the competition extends to proposed policies and ongoing projects, deeper down in the sites. In sum, the argument involves the worthiness of the collective, the capacity to study the issue lists (a shared format), and the distinctiveness of the collective's issues vis-à-vis its Web competitors, as well as the attractiveness of an approach with distance from its sources.

But we are also interested in the demystification of the aggregate. One rationale behind such an endeavor lies in the difficult and abstract subject

**Table 4.1**
Topics shared by leading issue portals; World Bank Development Gateway, Oneworld, and the UN, July 2001.

Topics shared by three leading issue portals; World Bank Development Gateway, Oneworld, and the UN, July 2001.

1. Agriculture
2. Indigenous Rights / Peoples / Knowledge / Health
3. Food / Food Safety
4. Education
5. Labour / Child Labour

Topics shared by at least two of the three leading issue portals; World Bank Development Gateway, Oneworld, and the UN.

1. Agriculture
2. Climate Change
3. Sustainable Development / Development Cooperation
4. Landmines / De-mining
5. Education
6. Indigenous
7. Environment
8. Energy
9. Human rights
10. Food
11. Children
12. Youth
13. Nuclear Issues / Atomic Energy
14. Disability
15. Refugees
16. Biodiversity
17. Trade / Trade Development
18. Democracy / Elections
19. Defense / Peace & Security
20. Population

matters at hand—global issues, globalization, global justice.[12] Asking an intuitively compelling basket of global civil society actors to tell us the (global) issues of collective significance—and determining when they are rising and falling in significance—provides balances and checks up on other reality-makers, as officialdom, the press, and even conventional press analysts.

Thus an important rationale behind the demystification exercise is to see whether that other, foggy picture of globalization emerging around world summits must continue to hold sway. In the newspapers and on the TV news we see tear gas, violent protest, "robocops," barricades, and death in the streets of Genoa.[13] Just beyond the press—in the intelligent weeklies and monthlies, and on such sites as mediachannel.org—we read analyses of mass media portrayals of the events. Summit reporting and analyses of summit media reporting have become a dominant story of globalization and anti-globalization. What are the pictures provided and how are they to be understood? Do these pictures of globalization square with the understandings provided by the Web and by the Web issue-makers?

To take up the critical analysis of issue representation, briefly, analyses of mass media coverage of Genoa and the preceding protest events in Quebec, Prague, Washington, D.C., and elsewhere dissect and disapprove of the dominant story line of the "few violent protestors spoiling it all" for the peaceful rest, and other often repeated lines and framings. Here is one example on Genoa media analysis, consisting of the main points of brief research into the biases in print and TV news reporting on Genoa. The analyst is attacking the assumptions feeding the pictures in the news and in our heads.

1. The first assumption is that the ruling class is peaceful. The protesters are violent.
2. The second assumption is that it is shocking when journalists are attacked (by the police) because they are innocent. By implication, all protesters are, if not guilty, than at least suspect and could well have deserved the beating they got.
3. The third assumption is that it is the right of the G8 powers to meet; the protesters have no right to be there.
4. The fourth assumption is that a minority causes violence.
5. The fifth assumption is that the protests aren't political. Real politics are conducted by world leaders only.[14]

Apart from dissecting bias in coverage, another large part of the media analysis around Genoa revolves around the rhetorical aspects of the debate spurred on by the events; that is, what is said about the protestors to the newspeople, how the protestors are branded. After all, the communicators must prepare positions, storylines, and quotations for the press. What is the line?

To take one example of such analysis, Susan George outlines three aspects of what may be termed the communication strategy of the summiteers and other pro-globalization forces.[15] These forces, we learn from George, are now dubbing the protesters "enemies of the poor," "unelected," and thereby "illegitimate" representatives of not the people but of "interest groups." The protesters also are ignorant and nonsensical in their ideas. She writes of insidious monitoring of the movement by such Internet surveillance contractors as eWatch, as well as the pulling of NGO funding by major foundations now under the influence of the conservatives. The overall point of the analysis is to lay bare the rhetoric fed to the mass media as well as the quiet corridor politics—that in fact we are dealing with competing issue-making tactics played out in the mass media and that there are dirty power plays in evidence behind the scenes. Finally, she issues a warning to the NGO community and the protesters to watch their backs.

If we may sum up the points made by the analysts, there are illegitimate framings behind the pictures we gain of the events from the mass media and their feeders, and these are made as if by disinformation tacticians. This is serious informational politics in action; it also quickly invites one to take sides, as many have, often unreasonably.[16]

One means to evaluate at least the framings of events is to put back into plain view the competition of our new issue-makers on the Web with another potential issue-maker, the press. In order to strengthen the argument and our interest in having Seattle or similar aggregations speak on their own terms or in our Issue Index terms, we may contrast sets of issues made around the Genoa G8 Summit in July of 2001. We compare those issues raised by two newspapers (the coverage) to those by the protest groups and by the summiteers (the competing sources). That is, we may make and compare issue lists from the "yellow zone" and the "red zone"—the places of the protesters and the summiteers at Genoa, respectively—and see whether and how they are covered in the newspapers. (Figure 4.5 is a map of Genoa made by local authorities, where

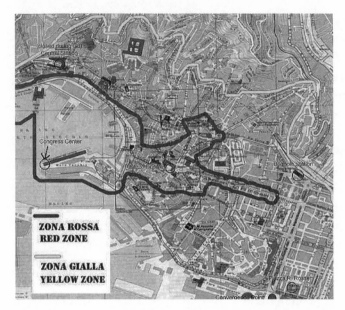

Figure 4.5
The red and the yellow zones in the city of Genoa, Italy, at the G8 Summit, July
20–22, 2001. Source: http://www.attac.de/genua/bilder/Seiten/ge_map.htm, captured on July 24, 2001.

the summit red zone and the protest yellow zone are depicted.[17]) Part of
any decision to take a side in the overall dispute—and to also make some
sense of the analysts' media assessments—are also matters of ascertaining whether there are competing realities on offer and whether there are
compelling and distinctive realities provided by each of our competitors.

## Issues at the Genoa G8 Summit: Comparing Online and Offline Newspaper Coverage

We watched the aftermath of the G8 Summit in Genoa on the Web (and
on TV and in the newspapers) during an issue mapping workshop in
Budapest. The exercise we undertook at the workshop a few days after
the completion of the summit was straightforward. We asked what are
the issues, according to the leading Web sites of the protesters and the
summiteers, and what are *their* respective issues according to selected
newspapers? Again we made issue lists, compared them, and drew some

preliminary conclusions. The findings would be of relevance not only to potential issue index-makers interested in the distinctiveness and demystification of organizations treating globalization, but also to those using the Web as reality check (as featured in chapter two), and to those evaluating whether the printed press or perhaps other starting points (for example, search engines) are to be the chosen inroads into issue networks on the Web (chapter three). While the above media analysts are mainly discussing coverage bias, standpoint engineering, and (serious) informational politics, the conclusions may be pertinent to them as well. Even if wide discrepancies between the mass media and the Web realities on offer were found, the point would not be to add fuel to debates about journalistic biases, driven by the pecuniary interests of media empires and other forces,[18] and introduce Indymedia alternatives, however valuable. Rather we are enquiring into the distinctiveness of a Web reality as a worthy competitor to the official reality-makers, in the sense put forward by C. Wright Mills:

In the absence of political debate that is wide and open and informed, people can get in touch neither with the effective realities of their world nor with the realities of themselves. Nowadays especially, it seems to me, the [public] role [of social science] I have been describing, requires no less than the presentation of conflicting definitions of reality itself. What is termed "propaganda" (. . .) consists not only of opinions on a variety of topics and issues. It is also the promulgation of official definitions of reality. Our public life now often rests on such official definitions, as well as upon myths and lies and crack-brained notions. When many policies—debated and undebated—are based on inadequate and misleading definitions of reality, then those who are out to define reality more adequately are bound to be unsettling influences.[19]

We would like to get to the heart of whether the various official definitions, especially of the yellow zone issues put forward by the newspapers and the summiteers, are indeed informed or crack-brained in the sense Wright Mills describes. But we also would like to raise the idea that the Web (as opposed to the media analysts of communication strategies we read about above) may serve as that valuable "unsettling influence." Thus, as we have done in preceding chapters, here too we introduce a medium and a Web analytical technique as the authors of a competing, unsettling reality.

Before we discuss the issue lists side by side, it should be mentioned that newspapers often have different print and online versions. To gain a grasp of the difference between the webby and the lesser webby worlds, it is instructive first to compare the link lists for Genoa stories provided by the offline *Der Standard* and its online version. (In their newspaper analysis, the researchers relied on two Austrian newspapers, the more respected *Der Standard* and the more popular *Die Kronen Zeitung*.) Typically, link lists serve as recommendations for further reading and research, but they also may be thought of as source checks and potential displays of journalistic knowledge, which may be a preferred link interpretation for these purposes.

In any event, the variation in the lists provided by the online and the offline papers is great, with the online version providing copious (and deep) links to the official summit site, three government sites, one mainstream media site, and numerous activist sites, while the print version furnishes a series of recommended sites that the online version does not find germane to understanding Genoa (such as the homepages of the WTO, IMF, World Bank, and the UN). Put differently, the print version could be said to ignore the reality of competition with the Web as well as that between the issue-makers on the Web (see table 4.2).

Looking at the link lists in more detail, side by side, one observation is that the print newspaper would be of scant aid in serving up starting points for entering the Web issue network around Genoa, a concern of the previous chapter. More telling to our current concerns is the skewing of the offline list of reader recommendations towards the intergovernmental sites (and shallow homepages). This finding prompted the researchers to raise the issue of the traditional standards of reliability and the channels upon which the printed press rely and continue to uphold, as if the Web is marginal. Moreover, our researchers wished to make an argument about the rise of digital journalism, where (perhaps contrary to the expectations of those seeing a merging of the offline and online worlds, allegedly owing to a commercialization and mainstreaming of the Web—remediation in a sense), the Web's new journalism, and presumably its outgoing stories and issue framings, would seem to diverge significantly from the offline's, at least in our small exercise in comparing source recommendations. (Thus one could find an argument here for aggregating Web stories and providing this new wire, as is already the case with the Web news aggregators discussed above.) The other major observation from comparisons of link lists is how irrelevant the online edition of *Der Standard* finds the Web sites of the intergovernmental organizations in the debate.

It is fair to remark that the print newspaper has not done its Web source homework, and that (digital) journalistic knowledge is not on display. Rejoinders about newspaper space constraints or old-fashioned editors would not alter an observation about distinctive digital journalism too greatly. To make a point stronger about separate story paths would require thorough comparisons of the online and offline versions of *Der Standard* around Genoa. But here we are still making a case in defence of a Web-only Issue Index, and in doing so we are in search of converging or diverging issue agendas on the part of the protesters, the summit participants, and the newspapers' coverage of them. Even if the offline newspaper is not recommending the sources online producers and audiences know are relevant and appropriate, *Der Standard*, and its popular counterpart, may very well be presenting the issues of the summit participants and the protestors.

The issue lists of the summiteers and the protestors are followed by those made (by our researchers) in the newspapers.

In an earlier demystification exercise surrounding the French farmer protests in June 2000, Noortje Marres and I were faced with newspapers calling the protesters "phony farmers" and "disorganized anarchists" on demo-holiday. We took *Le Monde* and *de Volkskrant* to task with a Web finding, using the issue network technique described in the previous chapter:

The farmers were not farmers, but represented an organizational figuration that moves from the national to the global and from the political-ideological to the issue-activist. [I]t is quite an organized picture, whereby neither farmers, nor "phony farmers," nor "a bunch of disorganized anarchists" make up the protests, but a professional national-international network.[20]

In the case of the French farmers we offer actor network ontologies and demonstrate the extent to which the Web could very well stretch the limits of reported reality of the identity of the protestors. In the Genoa case, we join with the previous research in asking whether the Web and Web collectives, perhaps counter-intuitively, are again closer to the streets (and to the conference tables) than the insider reporters and their stories. (Before undertaking the Genoa exercise, we had the suspicion that print journalists had caught up with digital journalism in understanding

**Table 4.2**
Comparison of G8 links provided by print and online versions of the Austrian newspaper *Der Standard*, July 19–26, 2001.

| G8 links provided by *Der Standard Online*, http://derstandard.at, July 19–26, 2001. | G8 links provided by the print newspaper (online), *Der Standard*, July 19–26, 2001. |
| --- | --- |
| Offizielle Seite zum Gipfel http://www.g8italia.it | Official G-8-Site http://www.g8italia.it |
| CNN-Special zum G8-Gipfel http://europe.cnn.com/SPECIAL S/2001/g8.summit | |
| Info-Website zum G8-Gipfel http://www.genoa-g8.it/eng/index.html | Zum Gegengipfel Weltsozialforum http://www.genoa-g8.org |
| Ministero del Commercio con l'Estero http://www.mincomes.it/compet enze/organig4.htm | |
| Italienisches Innen-ministerium http://www.cittadinitalia.it | |
| Bild des Schiffes, wo die Minister übernachten http://ilgiorno.monrif.net/ch an/speciale_g8:2322637:/2001/07/17 | |
| Gegen G8 http://www.controg8.org | |
| Genova Social Forum (GSF) http://www.genoa-g8.org/home.htm | |
| Deutsches Dokument des GSF http://www.genoa-g8.org/doc-ger.htm | |
| Independent Media Center, Italy http://italy.indymedia.org | |
| Attac http://www.attac-netzwerk.de | Attac http://www.attac.org |
| Menschen statt Profite www.menschenstattprofite.de | |
| Labournet www.labournet.de/diskussion/w ipo/seattle/genua.html | |
| Infohefte für die Proteste beim G8 Gipfel http://www.linksruck.de/rage/ material/0107genua_info.pdf | |

**Table 4.2**
(continued)

| G8 links provided by *Der Standard Online*, http://derstandard.at, July 19–26, 2001. | G8 links provided by the print newspaper (online), *Der Standard*, July 19–26, 2001. |
| --- | --- |
| Was geht ab in Genua? http://www.menschenvorprofite.de/ genua/genua.html | |
| Stadtpläne Genua http://www.attacnetzwerk.de/g enua/bilder/index.htm | |
| Freespeech http://free.freespeech.org/inter/genua | |
| Protest.net http://www.protest.net | |
| Bilder von den Sicherheits- vorkehrungen in Genua http://www.ecn.org/agp/g8genova/ indexpics.htm | |
| Tute bianche http://www.tutebianche.org | |
| Globalise resistance http://www.resist.org.uk | |
| Italienische Seite mit ausführlichen Nachrichten http://www.unimondo.org/genova2001 | |
| Seite mit weiteren Links http://www.ecn.org/g8 | |
| | Die Welthandelsorganisation WTO http://www.wto.org |
| | Weltbank http://www.worldbank.org |
| | Weltwährungsfond http://www.imf.org |
| | Die Vereinten Nationen http://www.un.org |

**Table 4.3**
G8 Summit Issues according to the Web sites of the summiteers and the protesters, July 19–26, 2001.

| Issues according to the summiteers in the Red Zone, July 19–26, 2001, http://www.genoa-g8.it[i] | Issues according to the protesters in the Yellow Zone (Rete Lilliput), July 19–26, 2001, http://www.retelilliput.org/g8/do cG8-en.asp[ii] |
|---|---|
| Debt relief | Debt cancellation for poor countries |
| Poverty, especially in Africa (and "making globalization work") | Native population and forest rights |
| Africa development plan (democratisation, conflict prevention and reduction, human development, particularly health and education, information and communication technology, the fight against corruption, stimulating private investment, increasing trade within Africa.)[iii] | Tax on international capital flows |
| | Ombudsman to arbiter IMF ctivities |
| | Export credit agencies reform. Blacklist credits for atomic research stations, garbage incinerators or thermoelectric installations that don't respect neither the highest standards about the energetic efficiency nor the progressive reduction of gases emissions; big dikes; the export of weapons, toxic and noxious substances not admitted by the International Conventions; the export of technology and products that could be used by police and military forces for repressive purposes and that could involve human rights violations (dual use goods); development projects or infrastructures in protected areas, natural reserves and parks that are not compatible with the park's purposes; new exploration and exploitation of fossil fuels (gas, oil, coal) projects in sensitive areas from a social and environmental point of |

| | view, such as virgin forests; extraction and processing activities on industrial scale of wood from virgin, tropical, boreal and temperate forests; infra structural project that would involve a forced evacuation of over 1000 people. White-list credits for projects and technologies with low-impact, such as renewable energetic sources on a small scale (fotovoltaico, geothermal, aeolian) |
| | Impact evaluation for other export credit agencies' projects |
| Kyoto mechanism (leaders divided) | National emission control policies |
| | No licenses granted on plants, animals and other living beings |
| | Genetic technologies (no patents on living organisms) |
| Global health fund | Stabilise prices of medicines in southern countries |
| Conflict resolution (former Yugoslavia, Macedonia, Middle East, Koreas) | Arms trade suspension with warring countries or with countries that do not respect human and civil rights |
| | Suspension of use of depleted uranium |
| | Institution of un-armed Peace Corps to be called in before any armed intervention |
| | Suspension of embargo against Iraq, except for military supplies |
| Digital divide | |
| Protest and implications for uture meetings (next summit in "remote Canadian Rockies, with smaller delegations") | |

i. See also http://www.genoa-g8.it/eng/summit/in_diretta/in_diretta_7.html, accessed in July 2001.

ii. See also http://www.genoa-g8.org, accessed in July 2001. "This web site offers information about a network of people and organizations who criticize today's world order, as unequal and unjust. It will do so in Genoa, during the G8 summit, on July 20–22, 2001." Previous network assemblies occurred in Seattle, Washington, DC, Bologna, Okinawa, Prague, Nice, Porto Alegre, and Napoli. The agenda of GSF's counter-summit ("Another World is Possible") is at http://www.genoa-3.g8.org/gpf-eng.htm, accessed in July 2001. http://www.genoa-g8.it/eng/summit/in_diretta/in_diretta_6.html, accessed in July 2001.

iii. http://www.genoa-g8.it/eng/summit/in_diretta/in_diretta_6.html, accessed in July 2001.

**Table 4.4**
G8 Summit Issues of the summiteers and the protesters according to *Die Kronen Zeitung* and *Der Standard*, July 19–26, 2001.

| Red Zone Issues<br>*Die Kronen Zeitung*<br>28 articles in 7 days,<br>July 19–26, 2001. | Yellow Zone Issues<br>*Die Kronen Zeitung*<br>28 articles in 7 days,<br>July 19–26, 2001. |
|---|---|
| Personal contact amongst the world's leaders | Distance of politicians from the people |
| The inclusion of the poorer countries in world summits | Poverty and exclusion |
|  | Wealth redistribution |
| Fight against poverty (through free trade) | World hunger |
| Energy and environment | Environmental exploitation |
| Trade relationships | Power of multinational companies |
|  | Anti-capitalism |
|  | Profit orientation |
|  | *Lobbyismus* |
|  | Concentration of power |
|  | Unemployment |
|  | Violence |
| Disarmament |  |
| Fight against organized crime |  |

| Red Zone Issues<br>*Der Standard*<br>66 Articles in 7 days,<br>July 19–26, 2001. | Yellow Zone Issues<br>*Der Standard*<br>66 Articles in 7 days,<br>July 19–26, 2001. |
|---|---|
| Drop the dept (and open markets for Third World products) | Debt elimination |
| Fight against poverty in non-developed countries (free trade) | Poverty |
|  | Anti-Free trade |
| Marshall Plan for Africa |  |
| Health fund (AIDS, TB) | Health (Asia, Africa) |
| Education and information technology |  |
| Wealth redistribution |  |
| Regulate globalization and international money markets | Tobin Tax |

**Table 4.4**
(continued)

| Red Zone Issues<br>*Der Standard*<br>66 Articles in 7 days,<br>July 19–26, 2001. | Yellow Zone Issues<br>*Der Standard*<br>66 Articles in 7 days,<br>July 19–26, 2001. |
| --- | --- |
| Kyoto | |
| GM food | |
| Missile defence system (USA vs. Russia) | |
| NATO expansion | |
| International terrorism | |
| International espionage | |
| Informal meetings, face-to-face talks | |
| Inclusion of protesters at summits | |
| | Police state militarism |
| | Child Labour |
| | Peace (in Chechnya) |
| | Anti-racism |
| | Refugees / Asylum policies |
| | Anti-globalization |
| | Decentralised network, universal movement |
| | Youthful idealism |
| | Anti-materialism |

professionalized networks of groups as the sources. But where *Der Standard* is concerned, this idea was not borne out in the link list comparisons.)

Now, in the Genoa research, we are keen to raise other prospects for the Web as issue-maker, in comparison with the newspapers (and also in preparation for the design of the new information stream). Does the Web exhibit an issue stability distinct from the well-known issue volatility of the newspaper?[21] If the answer is in the affirmative, we can begin making noises for a Web-driven information politics distinct from a mass-media-driven informational politics. Is it more specific? If it is both more stable and more specific, we can begin making reading recommendations for journalists and staffers to world leaders, not to mention many other followers of events and processes. There is another question, however, that is raised if we find issue stability and specificity on the Web. Does it lead us to unexpected ideas about real-time-ness, about news about issues? If issues are stickier and more durable on the Web than in the newspapers, we arrive at very different ideas about the consequences for print of Web and Internet information transmission speeds than we have held previously.[22] If the Web succeeds in competing with the press for recognition as issue-maker, does the Web show that issues do not come and go with the attention accorded to them by summit events (and newspaper coverage)?

Examining the issues lists, side by side, we may note that the popular newspaper, *Die Kronen Zeitung*, raises only a few of the larger issues and none of the specific issues or policy plans of the G8 summiteers. The more respected newspaper, *Der Standard*, engages in the summiteers' global issue specifics, albeit leaving out the conflict resolution issues. (Is it that all summits are now made into globalization—the historically minor departmental issues—as opposed to foreign affairs and major state departmental issues?) *Der Standard* also attempts to broaden the scope of the Summit, and indeed lectures world leaders about what they should be talking about, expanding the global issue list to include GM food, and also encouraging a regulation of globalization, as opposed to the summiteers' remarkable pronouncement of "making globalization work." (Next to the newspapers' and the protesters' issues and positions, the summiteers' statement startles for its nakedness. Without a more nuanced position on their part, it is as if the yellow zone outside the wall does not exist. Here we may recall Susan George's analysis of the communications strategy of the summiteers and the informational politics at work when the press reports the content of strategic communication as the news; if the protesters are branded illegitimate, then their views may be safely ignored.)

Turning to the yellow zone issues, our radar screens almost blacken. Both newspapers miss most of the Genoa issues, apart from *Der Standard*'s flagging of Tobin Tax and debt elimination for poor countries. We take notice of the treatment of activist culture in *Der Standard*'s talk of youthful idealism, but also its mention of the decentralized network with universalist ideas, mixing notions of social movements and issue networks. In all, with the newspapers out of touch with the current specifics of the yellow zone issues and mixing ideas about woollen socks with the observation about networks, we also cannot climb down from our previous speculation, based on the link list recommendations. The print newspaper has not caught up with digital journalism, not to mention with the Web as source, if one agrees (as we are increasingly finding) that the issues, positions, and culture of our new collective are really only explicable with an analysis of the new medium. They are certainly not in these newspapers.

More crucially, in just reading the newspapers we may miss the interaction between the issue lists of the summit participants and the protesters as well as the issues themselves. In any event, the world leaders and the activists are far apart, to put it as a newscaster may, not only on the approaches to specific issues (debt relief versus debt cancellation; emissions trading versus national emission limits) but also in the formulation of the agenda—the longer issue lists. Here it may be remarked that the range of issues, as well as the policy proposals put forward by the yellow zone, extend beyond what are becoming traditional globalization issues (for example, climate change) to geo-political and diplomatic considerations (peace-keeping policies). In general, one may be tempted to say their disagreements over the issue agendas and policies of the day, together with their being ignored, is why they are protesting. There's also the protest network culture, with movement momentum since Seattle as writers as Naomi Klein have discussed.[23]

From our brief research enterprise we have found some basis to defend the case for a Web Issue Index as a supplier of issues, issue lists (potential agendas), and policies distinct from more conventional issue-makers, such as the summiteers and the press.

But the Web seems to be taking us beyond journalism. Comparing issues made in the newspapers to those made by the summiteers and the protesters at Genoa assumed a kind of analytical symmetry of the media, new and old. Of course, we wanted to defend our case of the Web versus print and online journalism, but we did so with a particular point of departure—that they are in competition and that they should or must be compared. In doing so, we were quietly upholding a remediation thesis, as if new media were automating or digitizing the old. We could find reasons to defend a remediation thesis; there's plenty of typically formatted news stories on the Web, however much the sources feeding them may differ from the those of old media, as we found. But our results allow us to pursue different avenues of thought.

Susanna Hornig Priest has discussed the reality challenges put forward by the Web in the following terms, in connection with Internet campaigning against Monsanto's terminator gene in 1999.

Internet-based communications seemed to facilitate the spread of alternative and non-Western points of view in an era in which the activist press in the United States seems to have grown weak. Concerns that this technology has been colonized primarily by advertisers and marketers for their own purposes are well supported by the proliferation of public relations-oriented corporate Web sites, as well as sites specifically designed to sell products. But there can also be little doubt that Internet technology is filling part of the gap between the range of the opinions the U.S. press accommodates and the range that actually exists.[24]

An important rejoinder to the idea that the Web provides the range of opinions that actually exist would take into account a differentiation in the availability of that range owing to back-end and front-end politics; it also would account for Internet access issues, as well as (Web) media consumption habits and skills. Where the Web as competitor to informational politics is concerned (a view shared by Priest), there is the important issue of dominant search engine returns becoming aligned with highly mediated versionings of reality, a theme in chapter one (and in the concluding chapter). In other words, the opinions may be there, but how do we capture and display them? Our newspapers are not doing a very good job; Google, increasingly, is aligning with officialdom. It is in this context once more that we would defend our instrument as providing a remedy for informational politics.

There is an important parallel point being made about the shrinking exposure to a range of opinions as regards Web media consumption habits; it fits, too, with the Daily Me thesis. The *New York Times*, relying on marketing data and a study by the Pew Center, has reported a tendency in Web site visitation that shows that the accessed range is shrinking. Other scientists have found this as well.[25] Free-form browsing and searching are being displaced by habit (and apparently the tendencies of scale-free networks), as we also found, in chapter two, with regard to the preferences and routines of our research group looking up Viagra:

[N]ew data shows that for many people, the Web has become a routine electronic device. Often, Internet users stick to a half-dozen sites for news, sports scores, airline tickets and other things they need regularly. Many set up "personalized portals" that display only the categories of news, entertainment and financial information they are interested in when they log on.[26]

It should be mentioned that there is an assumption in these sorts of writings that derives from ideas of a "hit economy" as well as a free-for-all Web—that *all* sites are out to attract general audiences and general publics, and that it does not matter who visits, as long as there are many visits, preferably unique ones.[27] Thus it is worrying if people are increasingly visiting fewer sites. It is also a finding with serious consequences in terms of how the Web could ever compete with informational politics for the vast majority of habitual users. Additionally, it explains why Oneworld would desire to have its NGO issue news syndicated by Yahoo! news and placed in the list of world news feeds next to the Associated Press, Reuters, National Public Radio, and Agence France Presse—itself a great achievement. In designing the civil society issue stream, however, the initial questions relate to the necessity of competing with the press (and providing event news), as well as the eventual locations for the competing reality; that is, whether to secure them a place in the dominant portals.

### Beyond NGO news: Reformatting the Civil Society Issue Stream

The Web Issue Index assumes the form of an Issue Ticker.[28] Apart from a means to concentrate information and at once deepen it with multiple layers (as I will discuss), a ticker initially was chosen for two additional reasons; for its association with the .com boom period (where most commercial portals also would have a customisable MyStocks option) as well as for its expression of real-time-ness, a notion we shall be redefining with the aid of our issue-makers on the Web. To take up the first reason, one may take issue with the overall gravity as well as the normative consequences of an issue ticker. For example, it was learned that "allochtonen" (ethnicities) and "asylum seekers" are "declining issues" in the Echte Welvaart ticker, comparing basket data from March and May of 2001. This would not be such a palatable finding for many concerned; its explicit delivery in an information stream that harkens to the stock market—buying and selling behavior—is no less unsavory. The ticker could reek of the marketplace; it also could feed short-termism. The issue ticker, however, is a critical input; it puts on center stage the very idea of issue currency in a delivery form that is as literal as possible. It challenges the issue-making sources (and issue recipients) to review their own attention spans. More crucially, if single-issue movements are transforming into collectives for multiple issues, one may enquire into the collective's engagement drift—whether they drift from issue to issue depending on its currency, just like the newspapers and other currency markets generally do. Perhaps more startlingly, they may drift in concert with the issue agendas of inter-governmental organizations (as the UN or the World Bank), thereby collapsing the traditional distinction between civil society and the state.[29] Thus, from this particular perspective, the issue ticker is a self-exemplifying vehicle of critique.

Where the second reason is concerned, ticker streams capture one of the dominant forms of expression for currency, as is obvious, however much that currency varies according to access privileges. (One will be familiar with the 10-minute differences in delivery time between those paying for stock market streams and those accessing gratis ones.) In order to define currency for our ticker and thereby also the refresh rate (for example, every 10 minutes, daily, weekly, monthly), we have studied how frequently the collectives of NGOs refresh their issue lists. The good news from Genoa and the Web, if you will, has been the durability of issues, albeit with fluctuating sub-issues, as well as the pages most pointed to by the aggregated source sets per issue (our three layers). We have found that we need not constantly refresh; monthly refreshing for Seattle and bi-monthly for Echte Welvaart retains issue currency.

Apart from the rationale concerning the campaigners' Web issue activity, we have settled on these derived refresh rates in an attempt to contrast event and process. So far, we only noticed from our Genoa research that activist activity may be real-time for events. Is that activity per issue also event-based? If we had found that the baskets are news-driven and short-termist, then we could have safely abandoned the Web Issue Index of Civil Society and watched the NGO and Indymedia news aggregators only. Owing to the contrary finding, we have issue states and compositions instead of event news.

We have chosen to design issue states and compositions in the following manner: The Web Issue Index shows its state (rising, falling, stable) as well as the composition of issues in stacks. (See figure 4.6.) On the top level is the issues stream, the second layer the sub-issues (per issue), and the bottom layer is termed the "infoid." The notion of an

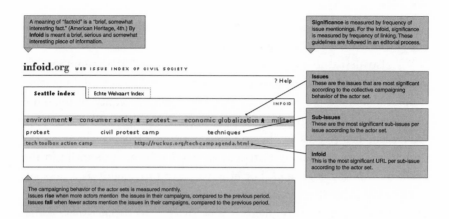

**Figure 4.6**
Design of infoid.org, version 1.0, with descriptions of the instrument. Design by Anderemedia.nl and the Govcom.org Foundation, Amsterdam. Programming of screensaver and application by Luke Pendrell and Martin Aberdeen. Data refresh by Greg Callman and Steffie Verstappen.

"infoid" has been created to convey a piece of information that tells a serious story, in the vein of the well-known word, factoid—a fact that often tells a trivial or silly story. (In referring to the work others call it an info ID—a system that provides information with an identity.)

In describing the infoid, we prefer the notion of a summarizing instantiation of an issue in the form of a piece of information. Consider an interest in the issue of climate change, note sub-issues such as "arctic meltdown" and "Pacific Islands in peril," and realize that the term demonstrating a summarizing instantiation of this issue is "Kirabatu," the country which has witnessed the disappearance of two of its small, uninhabited islands into the ocean.[30] A list of recalled consumer products containing StarLink corn, we thought, is an instantiation summarizing (at a particular moment in time) the genetically modified food issue. The analysis, in other words, is wading into the composition of the issue, providing current sub-issues and instantiations of them, the issue inputs that are contributing to the issue state. The design turns news upside down.

Just as importantly, the design leaves behind the flat, encyclopedic approach to information provision with a current and deeper issue compositional ontology. We propose the technique and the design as one means of capturing both the steady issue streams of civil society and the compositional inputs behind the state.

We also desire to put them on display, eventually, at summits. We would like it to be able to leave the confines of the Web as well. In putting it up at a summit, we propose to augment (summit) reality, in the sense discussed by Lev Manovich.[31] What is meant here is that the Web, as we have seen, has put us in the enviable position of being closer to the ground than eyewitness reporters and, thereby, being able to fill in the event *on top of the ground*. For now we have provided it as a desktop application as well as a screensaver, where the idea is to express our finding regarding stability: there is a persistence to social issues. If one ceases typing and mouse-clicking on the machine for ten minutes (the default activation setting), the issues return, fed to the desktop from a remote issue server. Penetrating the desktop, we thought, would allow us to avoid information formatting and (preferred) placement concerns encountered by those desiring inclusion in major portals (as in the Oneworld case).

By way of a conclusion, we would like to contrast the Issue Index with certain leading Web services that attempt to make people aware of information trends. In 2000 the Lycos search engine began a service showing the 50 most frequent queries made to the engine per week.[32] In 2001 Google began a similar query analysis service, with top 10 risers and decliners per week.[33] Yahoo! later added Buzz. To get a flavor of the week of July 16, 2001 (the Genoa G8 Summit period), we provide the information trends seen in Google's Zeitgeist and Lycos Top 50 services. (See tables 4.5 and 4.6.)

In Google's Zeitgeist a click on a term brings up a current Google engine query; in Lycos's top fifty, a click brings the user to the Lycos directory. For the presentation of the Issue Index here and by way of contrast between the different Web dynamics being captured, we have placed the issues in a similar style to the services, side by side. (See table 4.7.) The sites to be visited per issue appear below in the infoid table 4.8.

As alluded to above, we have found issue stability, with sub-issue and infoid fluctuation, over all the periods. The issue stream is distinctive in its substance from other issue portals as well as in its attention span (predictably, perhaps) to the press. Capturing and analyzing the campaigning lists of stable baskets of civil society actors has enabled us set up a stream of some interest for the press, the summit participants, and civil

**Table 4.5**
Google's Zeitgeist.

| Top 10 Gaining Queries—Week of July 16, 2001 | Top 10 Declining Queries—Week of July 16, 2001 |
| --- | --- |
| 1. chandra levy | 1. wimbledon |
| 2. final fantasy | 2. fireworks |
| 3. herman brood | 3. lichtallergie |
| 4. goran ivanisevic | 4. loft story |
| 5. big brother 2 | 5. msn messenger |
| 6. olympics | 6. AI |
| 7. reese witherspoon | 7. jim morrison |
| 8. emmy nominations | 8. jennifer capriati |
| 9. backstreet boys | 9. cricket |
| 10. kazaa | 10. madonna |

**Table 4.6**
Top Ten of Lycos 50.

Week ending July 14, 2001

1. Dragonball
9th week at #1

2. Big Brother
Controversial reality show

3. Britney Spears
Pop tart

4. Tour de France
Bike race

5. Tattoos
Skin is in

6. Final Fantasy
Movie tanks

7. IRS
Refunds coming

8. Napster
No music left

9. Pamela Anderson
Still hot

10. Morpheus
Hot music swap

**Table 4.7**
Web Issue Index of Civil Society, Seattle, Stream of July 15, 2001.

| Rising issues | Falling issues | Stable issues |
| --- | --- | --- |
| Global Trade Agreements | Social Security | Campaign Finance Reform |
| Health Care | Education | National Budget and Tax Policy |
| Biodiversity | Racial Equality | Occupational Health and Safety |
| Reproductive Rights | Religious Liberty | Students Rights |
| Water | Pay Equity | Work and Family |
| Global Warming | Environment and Population | Land Conservation/ Restoration |
| Labour and Rights | Cultural Diversity | Food Safety |
| Sweatshops | Privatization | Voting Rights |
| Genetic Engineering | Transgender Rights | Women's Rights |
| Drug Safety | Ecological Debt | Union Organization |
| Consumer Protection | Privacy | Animal Testing |
| Energy | Violence Against Women | Nuclear Waste |
| Sustainable Development | Independent Contractors | Rivers/Dams |
| Biotechnology | Homeless | Native Americans |
| US Military | | Resource Conservation |
| Protest Action | | Cyber Liberties |
| Law Enforcement | | Drug Policy |
| Free Speech Foreign Policy | | Clean Air |
| Prisons | | Pensions |
| Lesbian Gay Rights | | Unemployment |
| Immigration Rights | | Veterans |
| National Security | | Disabilities Rights |
| Policing Practices | | HIV-AIDS |
| | | Domestic Animals |
| | | Animals in Entertainment |
| | | Fur |

**Table 4.8**
Web Issue Index of Civil Society, Seattle Issues, Sub-issues and Infoids. Data in the first live stream of August 15, 2002.

| Status | Issue | Sub-issue | Infoid teaser text | Infoid URL |
|---|---|---|---|---|
| Stable | Animal Rights | Furs and Skins | Nonleather Shopping Guide | http://www.cowsarecool.com/altorders.asp |
| | Animal Rights | Vegan | Try the BK Veggie | http://www.peta.org/feat/bkveg/index.html |
| | Animal Rights | Animals in Entertainment | Sad Circus Elephant | http://www.circuses.com/aclu-dc.html |
| | Animal Rights | Pets | Dogs in Taiwan Desperately Need Help | http://peta.org/alert/automation/AlertItem.asp?id=374 |
| | Animal Rights | Horse Racing | Nike-Sponsored "Omak Suicide Race" | http://peta.org/alert/automation/AlertItem.asp?id=506 |
| | Animal Rights | Animal Testing | Caged Monkeys Protest March of Dimes | http://www.peta-online.org/news/NewsItem.asp?id=1190 |

**Table 4.8**
(continued)

| Status | Issue | Sub-issue | Infoid teaser text | Infoid URL |
|---|---|---|---|---|
| | Animal Rights | Pets | Dog Days of Summer Contest | http://www.peta.org/feat/dogcontest/index.html |
| Stable | Civil Rights | Voting Rights | Native American Litigation | http://www.aclu.org/news/2002/n080502a.html |
| | Civil Rights | Free Speech | The Judi Bari Homepage | http://www.judibari.org/ |
| | Civil Rights | Firearms | Beamhit: Marksmanship Training System | http://www.nra.org/modules/beamhit/190pmts.cfm |
| | Civil Rights | NRA | Message From Charlton Heston | http://www.nra.org/display_content/show_content.cfm?mod_id= 51&id=3750 |
| | Civil Rights | Firearms Lawsuits | Lawsuits Against Gun Manufacturers | http://www.nraila.org/Legislativedate.asp?FormMode= Detail&ID=447 |
| | Civil Rights | Privacy | Ashcroft and America's Most Wanted | http://www.aclu.org/tips/ |

| | | | | |
|---|---|---|---|---|
| | Civil Rights | Education | Florida's School Voucher Program | http://www.aclu.org/news/2002/n080502b.html |
| | Civil Rights | Prisoners' Rights | Sexual Slavery of Gay Black Man | http://www.aclu.org/features/f041802a.html |
| | Civil Rights | Freedom of Information | Australia and freedom of information | http://www.foei.org/cyberaction/calm.php |
| | Consumer Protection | Medicines | New Over the Counter Medicine Label | http://www.fda.gov/cder/consumerinfo/OTClabel.htm |
| Rising | Environment | Water | "Water For All" Program | http://www.citizen.org/cmep/Water/ |
| | Environment | Climate Change | Greenhouse Gas Emissions from Dams | http://www.irn.org/programs/greenhouse/index.asp?id=frontpage.html |
| | Environment | Corporate Responsibilty | Green Oscars, Vote Here | http://www.earthsummit.biz/awards/index.html |
| | Environment | Climate Change | Climate Change and the Great Lakes | http://www.nwf.org/climate/warmcoldfish.html |

**Table 4.8**
(continued)

| Status | Issue | Sub-issue | Infoid teaser text | Infoid URL |
|---|---|---|---|---|
| | Environment | Fish | Prevent Whirling Disease | http://www.nwf.org/climate/whirlingdisease.html |
| | Environment | Sprawl | Greening the Corps of Engineers | http://ga1.org/campaign/greeningcorps07102002?source=nwf_homepage |
| | Environment | Rain Forests | Join the RAN Journey to Amazonian Peru | http://www.ran.org/home/amazon_peru_trip.html |
| | Environment | Conservation Tours | Sierra Club Outings | http://www.sierraclub.org/outings/featured/index.asp |
| | Environment | Air Pollution | Hybrid Vehicles Replace SUVs | http://www.sierraclub.org/currents/last_excursion.asp |
| | Environment | Legislation | Congressional VoteWatch | http://www.sierraclub.org/votewatch/ |
| | Environment | Sprawl | Order a Free Sprawl Map | http://www.sierraclub.org/sprawl/report02/ |

| | | | |
|---|---|---|---|
| Environment | Energy | The Online Energy Forum | http://www.sierraclub.org/powerlunch/ |
| Environment | Recreation | Proper Hiking with Your Dog | http://www.sierraclub.org/e-files/dog_hiking.asp |
| Environment | Forests | No New Wilderness for Tongass | http://www.wilderness.org/takeaction/?step=2&item=1774 |
| Environment | Rivers | Protect the Grand Canyon River | http://www.wilderness.org/takeaction/?step=2&item=1768 |
| Environment | Forests | What's Burning Now? | http://www.nifc.gov/fireinfo/nfn.html |
| Environment | Oil | Changing Oil: Online Book | http://capmarkets.wri.org/publication_pdf.cfm?PubID=3719 |
| Environment | Energy | Power Politics: Online Book | http://www.wri.org/wri/governance/powerpolitics_toc.html |
| Environment | Information | Environmental Information Portal | http://earthtrends.wri.org/ |
| Environment | Central Asia | Environment Profiles | http://www.wri.org/wri/central_asia/country_profiles.html |
| Environment | Central Asia | Watershed Profiles | http://www.wri.org/wri/central_asia/watersheds.html |

**Table 4.8**
(continued)

| Status | Issue | Sub-issue | Infoid teaser text | Infoid URL |
|---|---|---|---|---|
|  | Environment | Chemical Pollution | Hormone Mimicking Chemicals | http://www.panda.org/news/press/news.cfm?id=3075 |
|  | Environment | Forests | Make NYC Use Eco-Wood | http://passport.panda.org/campaign/index.cfm?campaign=2157&lang=13&campaign_lang=13 |
|  | Environment | Climate Change | Go for Kyoto Campaign | http://www.panda.org/goforkyoto/ |
|  | Environment | Oceans | The Living Website | http://passport.panda.org/stopoverfishing/html//livingwebsite/livingwebsite.cfm |
|  | Environment | Fishing | Stop Over Fishing | http://passport.panda.org/stopoverfishing/html/fishingmadness/fishingmadness.cfm |
|  | Environment | Fundraising | Run the Tahiti Marathon! | http://www.tahitimarathon.com/ |
|  | Environment | Endangered Species | Polar Bear Tracker | http://www.panda.org/polarbears/ |
|  | Environment | Fish | Guide to Responsible Eating | http://www.enature.com/feature/feature_news.zasp?storyID=509 |

| Category | Subcategory | | Title | URL |
|---|---|---|---|---|
| Environment | Forests | | | |
| | | Rising | National Fire Weather Forecasts | http://www.boi.noaa.gov/firewx.htm |
| Global Economy | Johannesburg Summit | | World Summit Tour | http://www.globalexchange.org/tours/auto/2002-08-22_WorldSummitonSustainableDevel.html |
| Global Economy | FTAA | | Truth and Consequences Tour | http://www.globalexchange.org/tours/auto/2002-10-23_FTAATruthConsequences.html |
| Global Economy | Sustainable Development | | Attend The Green Festival | http://www.greenfestivals.com/l |
| Global Economy | Corporate Responsibilty | | Corporate Crime Center | http://www.citizen.org/_corpcrime/articles.cfm?ID=8075 |
| Global Economy | Development | | IMF's Financial Arrangements | http://www.imf.org/external/np/tre/activity/2002/080902.htm#tab2a |
| Global Economy | Tobacco | | Economics of Tobacco Control | http://www1.worldbank.org/tobacco/ |
| Global Economy | Fair Trade | | StarBucks on Fair Trade | http://www.starbucks.com/aboutus/gmo_date.asp |
| Global Economy | Poverty Reduction | | Yemen's Strategy | http://poverty.worldbank.org/files/Yemen_PRSP.pdf |
| Global Economy | Emergency Financial Support | | World Bank's Brazil Highlights | http://lnweb18.worldbank.org/External/lac/lac.nsf/4c794feb793085a5852567d600 |

**Table 4.8**
(continued)

| Status | Issue | Sub-issue | Infoid teaser text | Infoid URL |
|---|---|---|---|---|
| | Global Economy | Development | World Bank's Pakistan Profile | http://devdata.worldbank.org/external/CPProfile.asp?SelectedCountry=PAK&CCODE=PAK&CNAME=Pakistan&PTYPE=CP |
| | Global Economy | Transparency | Information Disclosure | http://www1.worldbank.org/operations/disclosure/ |
| | Global Economy | Development | New Opportunity for Kosovo | http://web.worldbank.org/WBSITE/EXTERNAL/NEWS/0,,contentMDK:20058331~menK:34457~pagePK:34370~piPK:42768~theSitePK:4607,00.htm |
| | Global Economy | Development | The World Bank in Afghanistan | http://lnweb18.worldbank.org/sar/sa.nsf/Afghanistan?OpenNavigator |
| | Global Economy | WTO | The Doha Agenda | http://www.wto.org/english/tratop_e/dda_e/dda_e.htm |
| | Global Economy | Corporate Accountability | Stanley Works' Mail Box in Bermuda | http://www.aflcio.org/news/2002/0802_stanley.htm |
| | Global Economy | Corporate Responsibility | Boise's statements with SEC | http://www.bc.com/ |

| | | | | |
|---|---|---|---|---|
| | Global Economy | NAFTA | California's Ban on MTBE | http://www.citizen.org/hot_issues/issue.cfm?ID=354 |
| | Global Economy | Fast Track | Bush's Fast Track Backward | http://www.citizen.org/pressroom/release.cfm?ID=1177 |
| Falling | Health | Auto Safety | Nissan Ultima Airbags | http://www.citizen.org/autosafety/Air_Bags/nissanaltima/ |
| | Health | Consumer Protection | Constipation treatment for women | http://www.fda.gov/bbs/topics/ANSWERS/2002/ANS01160.html |
| | Heath | Medical Products | Testicular Prosthesis | http://www.fda.gov/cdrh/mda/docs/p020003.pdf |
| Stable | Protest Action | Online Resources | Anarchist Guide to Critical Thinking | http://www.infoshop.org/critical_thinking.html |
| | Protest Action | Camps | Ruckus Society Tech Action Camp | http://ruckus.org/training/techcamp/index.html |
| | Protest Action | Democracy | Rolling Thunder Democracy Tour | http://www.rollingthundertour.org/ |

**Table 4.8**
(continued)

| Status | Issue | Sub-issue | Infoid teaser text | Infoid URL |
|---|---|---|---|---|
| Rising | Terrorism | Afghanistan | Discover Afghan Heritage Tour | http://www.globalexchange.org/tours/auto/2002-09-08_DiscoverAfghanHeritage.html |
| | Terrorism | Counter Terrorism Strategies | Terrorist Finance | http://www.imf.org/external/np/sec/pn/2002/pn0287.htm |
| | Terrorism | Air Transportation | Armed Pilots | http://www.nraila.org/Legislativedate.asp?FormMode=Detail&ID=440 |
| Rising | Workers Rights | Pay Equity | Play "Take the Money and Run" | http://www.aflcio.org/paywatch/takeandrun.swf |
| | Workers Rights | Sweatshops | Buy Union, Online Shop | http://www.uniteunion.org/unionlabel/ |
| | Workers Rights | Legislation | The Bush Watch | http://www.aflcio.org/bushwatch/index.htm |
| | Workers Rights | Labor Solidarity | Corvette Turns 50 | http://www.uaw.org/solidarity/02/0802/feature03.cfm |

society. More importantly, the stream and especially the technique aim to provide some measure of remedy to informational politics (through the screensaver's persistence) and eventually to augment the reality on the ground.

## Appendixes

### Appendix 4.1    Organizations comprising the Echte Welvaart Basket, 2002–2003

| | |
|---|---|
| Algemene Vergadering Verplegenden en Verzorgenden | http://www.avvv.nl |
| Alternatieve Konsumentenbond | http://www.pz.nl/akb |
| ANBO de Bond voor 50-plussers | http://www.seniorweb.nl/anbo |
| Consumentenbond | http://www.consumentenbond.nl |
| FNV | http://www.fnv.nl |
| In Natura | http://www.ltonet.nl/wlto |
| IVN Vereniging voor Natuur en milieueducatie | http://www.ivn.nl |
| Landelijk Centrum Opbouwwerk | http://www.opbouwwerk.nl |
| Landschapsbeheer Nederland | http://www.landschapsbeheer.nl |
| Nationale Jongerenraad voor Milieu en Ontwikkeling | http://www.njmo.nl |
| Nederlandse Bond voor Plattelandsvrouwen | http://www.nbvp.nl |
| Nederlandse Politiebond | http://www.politiebond.nl |
| Nederlandse Vereniging tot Bescherming van Dieren | http://www.dierenbescherming.nl |
| NIVON | http://www.nivon.nl |
| Novib | http://www.novib.nl |
| Raad van Kerken | http://www.raadvankerken.nl |
| Stichting Natuur en Milieu | http://www.snm.nl |
| Vastenaktie | http://www.vastenaktie.nl |
| Vereniging Milieudefensie | http://www.milieudefensie.nl |
| Vereniging Natuurmonumenten | http://www.natuurmonumenten.nl |
| Vereniging Nederlandse Vrouwen Raad | http://www.vrouwen.net/nvr |
| Koninklijke Nederlandse Maatschappij ter bevordering der Geneeskunst | http://www.knmg.nl |

Vereniging Nederlandse                http://www.npcf.nl
Patienten/Consumenten
Federatie

Humanistisch Verbond                  http://www.humanistischverbond.nl
Vluchtelingen Organisaties            http://www.
                                      vluchtelingenorganisaties.nl
Nederland

Instituut voor Multiculturele         http://www.forum.nl
Ontwikkeling


**Appendix 4.2    Organizations comprising the Seattle Basket,
2002–2003**

| | |
|---|---|
| American Civil Liberties Union | http://www.aclu.org |
| ACT UP | http://www.actupny.org |
| AFL-CIO | http://www.aflcio.org |
| American Federation of State, County and Municipal Employees | http://www.afscme.org |
| Alliance for Sustainable Jobs and the Enviroinment | http://www.asje.org |
| Black Bloc | http://www.infoshop.org |
| Boise Cascade Corp. | http://www.bc.com |
| Confederation Paysanne | http://confederationpaysanne.fr |
| Critical Mass | http://www.criticalmass.org |
| Direct Action Network | http://dan.raisethefist.com |
| Earth First! | http://www.earthfirst.org |
| Earth Island Institute | http://www.earthisland.org |
| EcoRopa | http://www.ecoropa.org |
| Federal Communications Commission | http://www.fcc.gov |
| Food and Drug Administration | http://www.fda.gov |
| Food Not Bombs | http://www.scn.org/foodnotbombs |
| Friends of the Earth | http://www.foei.org |
| Global Exchange | http://www.globalexchange.org |
| Global Trade Watch | http://www.tradewatch.org |
| International Brotherhood of Electrical Workers | http://www.ibew.org |
| Independent Media Center | http://www.indymedia.org |
| Inlandboatmen's Union | http://www.ibu.org |

| | |
|---|---|
| International Forum on Globalization | http://www.ifg.org |
| International Monetary Fund | http://www.imf.org |
| International Rivers Network | http://www.irn.org |
| Jobs with Justice | http://www.jwj.org |
| Jubilee 2000 | http://www.j2000usa.org |
| International Longshoremen | http://www.ila2000.org |
| International Assoc. of Machinists and Aerospace Workers | http://www.iamaw.org |
| Monsanto Corp. | http://www.monsanto.com |
| National Lawyers Guild | http://www.nlg.org |
| National Rifle Association | http://www.nra.org |
| National Wildlife Federation | http://www.nwf.org |
| Nike Corp. | http://www.nike.com |
| Novartis Corp. | http://www.novartis.com |
| Occidental Petroleum | http://www.oxy.com |
| Oil, Chemical & Atomic Workers | http://www.webshells.com/ocaw |
| Organization of American States | http://www.oas.org |
| People for the Ethical Treatment of Animals | http://www.peta-online.org |
| Press for Change | http://www.pfc.org.uk |
| PureFood Campaign | http://www.purefood.org |
| Rainforest Action Network | http://www.ran.org |
| Ruckus Society | http://ruckus.org |
| Sierra Club | http://www.sierraclub.org |
| Starbucks Corp. | http://www.starbucks.com |
| United Autoworkers | http://www.uaw.org |
| United Students Against Sweatshops | http://www.usasnet.org |
| United Steelworkers of America | http://www.uswa.org |
| UNITE | http://www.uniteunion.org |
| Wilderness Society | http://www.wilderness.org |
| World Bank | http://www.worldbank.org |
| World Resources Institute | http://www.wri.org/wri |
| World Trade Organization | http://www.wto.org |
| World Wildlife Fund | http://www.panda.org |

# 5

# Election Issue Tracker: Monitoring the Politics of Attention

## Introduction

The previous chapter was an attempt to defend the creation, as well as a particular design, of a dedicated civil society issue stream. This defense of the creation of a dedicated stream rested on empirical findings concerning the inadequacies of coverage of the civil society issues by the press as well as the summiteers at G8 in Genoa. The findings also led to an additional item of interest to many curious about Web source dynamics vis-à-vis print media; that is, the relative stability of issues on civil society sites (those found in the Seattle and Echte Welvaart source baskets). We found streams need not be refreshed daily; monthly or bi-monthly queries will do. Thus the news about civil society issue-making is that it follows an attention cycle quite distinct from the press. This allowed the researchers and me to propose an information design different from that of the existing NGO issue and news portals, as at Oneworld or Indymedia. Here we shall continue those thoughts about press attention to issues, and inquire into whether we can now thrust our information politics into a realm dominated by informational politics, the elections. We are interested in looking into relationships between news coverage and party issue politics in the run up to national elections. There is much at stake.

We are back on Dutch soil, where a national election is about to take place. The political parties are publishing their platforms, and other social groups are coming forward with their issues and views as well. We would like to design a system that displays how the issues of the parties, as well as those of the social groups, are resonating in the press. More importantly, we are interested in how press attention to issues may be affecting the behavior of the parties and the groups; whether they are in sync with the news, whether press coverage is over-determining party-political attention to issues, and whether we can put on display the scope of informational politics at work at the time one would expect it the most.

As mentioned in chapter one, the application we wish to put forward is distinct in spirit from the previous ones. The instruments described in chapters two, three, and four have employed the Web, and the particular (crossed) information streams derived from it, as different kinds of reality checks and eye-openers for government as well as the other individuals and groups that have been identified, mapped, and streamed—largely NGOs and street culture but also their informational relationships with officialdom. Here we step backstage and look into how political strategists (not to mention other issue-makers and issue-watchers) may be dealing with press attention. Ours is an instrument that raises dilemmas about watching the press in a particular way to gain indications of how well or poorly a party and its issues are doing from a press publicity point of view. Briefly, the stream attempts to capture and display a politics of press attention.

In order to do so, we find a means of grabbing issues and querying the press for their respective resonance. Of equal significance, we also find a means of differentiating between issues and non-issues prior to querying the press. The first half of the chapter presents the heuristic and the method employed to measure attention accorded to issues and non-issues. It also provides arguments about how to organize the new attention stream—whether or not to pre-classify and categorize, for example, along the lines of ministerial responsibility (as mentioned in chapter one in the UK online Citizens portal and in chapter three in the case of the Dutch government's tidying of the nuclear energy debate). Once we have done so, we present some of the findings that pose dilemmas for political parties and social groups in their substantive relations with the press. Ultimately, with the aid of the instrument and its findings, we will approach the question of how can one tell when politics are press-driven. How can one tell whether an informational politics is being put into practice? May there be a measure of remedy offered through our Web epistemological practice?

## Non-issue.nl: The Purpose of the Election Issue Tracker

The purpose of non-issue.nl (our project name) is to identify election issues and then chart the changing press attention to them over time.[1] We identify and monitor the political parties' election issues as well as what we dub election non-issues; that is, those issues from an aggregation of Dutch NGOs not appearing on party platforms.

In the Election Issue Tracker (the outcome of the project), we compare the resonance of the issues and the non-issues by measuring issue "terminological currency" over time across three leading national newspapers: *de Volkskrant, de Telegraaf,* and the *NRC Handelsblad.* Resonance per issue is defined, straightforwardly, as frequency of mentions of the issue terms per newspaper and across newspapers. (See figure 5.1.)

Issues are taken directly from party platforms.[2] Normally, the issues are ascertained by seeking summaries of the party's ambitions—bullet points in the platform that sum up the issues and the party's positions on them. Single issue lists are derived from the summaries. These are issue key words (singlets or couplets) that are specific enough, terminologically, to stand out from broader topics in large collections of press articles. For example, "waiting lists" could be defined as an issue within (or under) the topic of "health care." In that case, we would use the system to first search for "waiting lists," and then collect those "waiting list" returns having to do with health care. We also could check whether "waiting lists" is migrating to other topics; issues may heat up (we believe) when certain terms become attached to them.

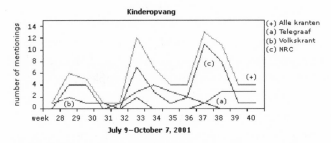

**Figure 5.1**
Press Issue Attention Graph for Kinderopvang (child care), an issue on the platform of the PvdA (Labour Party). Modified MS-Excel graph.

This sorting work we view as a pragmatic heuristic, more in the bottom-up "bag theory" school of classification than the top-down Aristotilean.[3] With this heuristic we need not specify in advance what sections of the newspapers we are searching. We query the entire newspaper database (over particular time frames) for each of the key words, bring back all results, and then search within them to seek their relative topicality.

Before returning to how and why we monitor issues, we would like to explain why we do not analytically pre-classify in our sorting work—why we rather would allow the issues to leave pre-set categories, migrate, and make other topics hot by attaching themselves to the terms of the moment. In contrast, a newspaper generally analytically pre-classifies by separating news into departments—national, international, etc., corresponding to the different desks. Similarly, when a book arrives at a library, there is the question of the section and sub-section to which it belongs—reference, fiction, non-fiction, and the further sub-classes. (Only certain special collections un-classify, holding all subject-area books, no matter what the genre, in one place.)

Here we do not know in advance where issues belong, whether they should be pre-classified according to the subjects dealt with by the newspaper desks, by the library science classification schemes, or, as mentioned, by the division of issue responsibility by individual ministries. We prefer to allow the issues to shape the categorizations; we only know that we should follow the current terms, watching whether they stick themselves to ministries and parties, as well as other issues. Thus our issue stream will be without a prior classification scheme apart from currency and attention (which we define below).

There are two reasons for such a non-analytical approach. First, we seek to make a political instrument. As such, one prefers to politicize through pinpointing and watching narrow terminological issues, rather than to de-politicize by seeking and watching generic topics. Second, following the narrower terms allows us to seek currency in seminal ways. We mean this in two senses. The first sense is the straightforward counting of mentions of specific terms as opposed to broad ones. Specific terms allow one to enjoy the spikes, see hype come and go, name it as such, disagree with its characterization, recommend a term to a topic in need of it—help make an issue an issue, perhaps. (For example, "conflict diamonds," previously known as blood diamonds for their association with financing war, has aided the logging issue recently through the coinage of "conflict timber.")

One of the project researchers asked whether we should group together issues that parties are using by different terms. Surely the parties are talking about the same thing, but in different language. We refrained not only because such translations are the job of the parties (perhaps as a result of their press monitoring), but also more importantly because we wish to see when they begin using the same terms (and whether they all begin simultaneously). In the second sense, we are watching the arrival and departure of words that may defy previous classification or may be in need of fresh ones. For example, a debate (in the Dutch government-organized sense) took place in the 1990s around "mobility." Holding the debate was (among other things) a terminological move; it was an attempt to move the debate to another level of abstraction for a number of reasons, including the encouragement of creativity (by the citizens and social groups involved) in finding new, broader policies—ones that could swallow (in a sense) vociferous winnowed issue debates around the fifth runway now opened at Schiphol airport or the new freight line (Betuwelijn) through the green heart of the country. As mentioned in chapter three, normally policy-making is a process of narrowing, not broadening, unless, as is our task, to seek emergent issues and emergent framings. With mobility we have witnessed a case of government allowing the terms, issues, and policies to attach themselves to mobility. A mobility debate also would be more intellectually engaging, perhaps, than a runway debate. These days, however, mobility as an issue no longer appears on the platforms. As important as it may be, the term has had its day, politically. The same holds (for certain parties) for sustainable development, but "sustainable" has shown resilience, having migrated to other terms and connecting itself with issues, perhaps helping to make them. We are interested in the currency of terms, for they tell us more about attention and lifespans of issues than pre-classified topics arranged by ministerial responsibility, newspaper desk, or library. They also show us when political issues die through terminological work.

## Defining the Non-issues

Once definitive party issue lists are defined (our terms), each issue's relative press currency is sought. To find it, we search the archives of three leading Dutch newspapers (*de Volkskrant, NRC Handelsblad*, and *de Telegraaf*), available in digital form in dedicated databases on the Web.[4] Once queried, we start counting mentions by date. Technical and methodological difficulties arise in querying the digital over the print and collating the data returned to compare like with like. Where the difficulties are concerned, one question revolves around the contents of the archives and whether it makes much difference to the undertaking whether the techniques applied in conventional newspaper analyses are unavailable. Another way of phrasing the question is, can we make do with the text that (in two of our three cases) is freely available on the Web? (We had to take out a subscription to the *NRC Handelsblad* to count their term mentions in the digital archive.) For example, headline size, department of newspaper (with one exception), page number, column inches, name of journalist, story type (news, editorial, etc.) and many other possible inputs for well-known metrics are not provided. For terminological and other analyses, other telling items such as advertisements are also not returned; in the digital archives there is not a diagram, infographic, or table in sight—only the text of the articles without the rest of the paper.[5]

The databases are organized in ways that return up to seven information fields: headline (all three newspapers), date (all), dateline or city (*Telegraaf* only), newspaper desk or department (*NRC* only), word count (*Volkskrant* and *NRC*), the first few lines of article otherwise known as "teaser text" (all), and key words (*NRC* only). (See example of archive returns in table 5.1 for the query "child care," or *kinderopvang*.)

Asymmetries in (digital and print) archive organization are not uncommon, despite well-adopted standards. We have been forced, for comparative purposes, to use the lowest common denominator—headline, date, and article text. Working with these fields only, we seek to derive some measure of press attention to issues. We could have boosted the ranking of a term (in various ways) if it had appeared in a headline; indeed, we could count headline terms only, and declare relative attention that way. Instead we keep to a general heuristic applied throughout our

**Table 5.1**
Sample Newspaper Archive Returns.

---

*De Telegraaf*
Kinderopvang 9 procent duurder
8 jan. 2002
AMSTERDAM—*Kinderopvang* is vorig jaar negen procent duurder geworden.
Dit maakte Kintent, uitvoerder van bedrijfs*kinderopvang* gisteren bekend. Een
volledige plaats voor een kind op een crèche of andere vorm van opvang
kostte in 2001 . . . (bron: archief)

*De Volkskrant*
Staking in kinderopvang
Woensdag 9 januari 2002 (188 woorden)
—Abvakabo- onderhandelaar J. Dieten schat dat woensdag bij circa 230
kinderopvangcentra in meer of mindere mate wordt gestaakt. Donderdag legt
het personeel bij . . .

*NRC Handelsblad*
Kindercentra gesloten door CAO-conflict
Binnenland, woensdag 9 januari (309 woorden)
De AbvaKabo schat dat er vandaag bij 230 kindercentra in meer of mindere
mate is gestaakt. Donderdag wordt er bij zeventig andere centra gestaakt. Het
is inmiddels voor de vierde keer in korte tijd dat er in de kinderopvang wordt
gestaakt. Trefwoorden Economie, Maatschappij, Sociale economie,
Arbeidsvoorwaarden, Arbeidsonrust, Welzijn, Kinderopvang

---

Archives return:
Name of newspaper (all)
Article headline (all)
Article date (all)
Word count (*De Volkskrant* and *NRC Handelslad*)
Teaser text (all)
Key words (*NRC Handelsblad*)
Newspaper section (*NRC Handelsblad*)
Digital source (*De Telegraaf*)

instrumention design (following the Web information available), and make use of the returns in the stream form in which they are furnished to us. We mean (fortunately) that all of the newspapers do not double count terms if they appear in the text and the headline (or more than once in the text). Frequency of mentions is a measure of single articles— one mention is one article. We are now allowed to provide a definition of press attention. Attention is defined as the number of articles in which the issue term is mentioned. We believe this to be a more robust metric for attention than an overall mentions count or a term-in-headline count.

There are two other (technical) lowest common denominators that we have been forced to use, and are still happy with. The *NRC Handelsblad* only takes single key word queries. Thus (in the batch query system we devised) all our queries must be single words. We subsequently seek couplets—*groene stroom* (green current), for example—within the individual stories returned. Also, the *NRC Handelsblad* returns articles only over the previous three months. Our system thus shows currency over the past three months. But we also are saving the results on a daily basis, thereby adding to current public domain information (previously) furnished by the *NRC* on any given date.

The Web Issue Index (chapter four) provides continually refreshed issue lists from a cross-section of Dutch NGOs. The Echte Welvaart Index—the abstract, multi-issue movement—provides telling variations in rising and falling issues of collective NGO concern, so we make use of it. In the Election Issue Tracker we compare the political party issue lists with that of the current NGOs' in Echte Welvaart, seeking matches. The NGOs may be campaigning for some of the same issues, terminologically speaking. They may have others. The NGO campaign issues not on the party platform lists—the non-matches—are dubbed the election non-issues. The currency of the non-issues is charted in the same way as the currency of the issues, by querying the newspapers and counting the frequency of mentions of the issue terms over time (as above). This way one can chart and compare the resonance of party election issues and non-issues in the newspapers in the run-up to the national election.

Using NGO campaigns for making comparisons between issues and non-issues relies on a few observations, some of which have made previously. First, we employ the term election non-issue somewhat provocatively, meaning an issue of measurable social concern not addressed by party election platforms. To lead us to these election non-issues we prefer what could be called *everyday issue professionals* (the NGOs) over, for example, the public (or, more fashionably, "publics") brought to life by the press or government by polling or placing newspaper advertisements for concerned citizens to attend a public debate, as mentioned in chapter three. Here we could begin a discussion about methodological opportunism and constructing doability—about the relative ease of sampling NGO campaigns and deriving issue lists from them versus setting up the apparatus to measure the concerns of publics (as in telephone polling with propensity weighting), or going the further step of measuring those of informed publics (as in deliberative polling or sophisticated public debate techniques).[6] Criticisms may be raised about our approach. While informed, the NGOs may be discounted as interested (or, worse still, lobbying) parties. The public debate technicians (who place the newspaper ads inviting citizens to come forward for a public debate) also are aware of this. The more sophisticated public debate procedures attempt to have the social groups first put their interests on the table, and then engage in forms of reflexive social learning whereby the groups realize they can learn to move beyond self-interest.

To allay such concerns we wish to recall that the NGOs are not being invited (in a voluntaristic procedure of public debate or deliberative polling) to defend their interests in the public domain. Instead of taking the pains to put into place a performative procedure (and begin a round of arguments about the extent to which these organizations are actually engaging in reflexive social learning), we shall state that the NGOs are unaware of our measures and may carry on as usual. As argued in the introduction, we would prefer that everyday behavior over performance at roundtables. Furthermore, we believe the everyday behavior is more telling of what could well happen once the public debate procedure has concluded and the social groups are no longer under the pressure to learn, to be reflexive, and to perform.

Significantly, we also are interested in gauging issues of social concern through the press. In the previous chapter we discussed the distinctiveness of the NGO issue streams—that they are distinctive as well as worthy enough to merit a separate stream, as, in a similar sense, blogs now have their own aggregated streams delivered by technorati.com and daypop.com. The point in chapter four was to show how the press (and official G8 summit sites) is not adequately capturing the NGO issues; with the Web Issue Index we invited them to augment their reality. Not discussed in the previous chapter was the great tragedy of NGO relations with the government and the press. While critical of press story framings (and also sure to address other network actors in their view releases), NGOs are in the business of attracting press coverage. Besides membership figures (donations or magazine subscriptions), coverage is also a measure of success, how well they are doing. (Funders, other media, and even government may take more notice.) They even proudly link to coverage. Thus our issue professionals are more likely to devise press penetration strategies than others (citizens, publics, etc.) more remotely concerned with issues in a professional sense. When NGO issues are not picked up in the press (despite NGO press strategies and NGO press savviness), we are better able to call these non-issues—issues defined as such by professionals, put forward in press strategies, but currently denied press attention.

The issue currency streams are utilised to note the dynamics between (print and NGO) press and party issue formations and the print and Web conditions under which any changes are made to party issue lists, as well as to NGO lists. Here the aim would be to gain an idea of the extent to which sources drive issues or issues drive sources. More broadly put, when and under which conditions are political party election agendas driven by civil society, the press, or by other parties? With the Election Issue Tracker (combined with the Web Issue Index), one is able to chart newspaper attention to party and to NGO issues over time, to chart party attention to NGO issues, and to chart NGO attention to party issues. (Below we discuss why we use the press for issue currency only, and not for issue identification.)

**Information Stream Design and Info-political Research**

We have conceived an issue currency monitoring system. The Election Issue Tracker is conceived in terms of a news-about-news space, borrowing its style initially from a business news TV-portal, but without the talking head(s). (Later, and perhaps more accurately, others thought the instrument looked like a transportation monitoring system, adding to the work the idea that we in fact are watching issue transport.)

Running at the top of the space is the issue streamer—all of the issues of the parties and the NGOs in one stream. Following the non-analytical or non-classifing approach defended above, the issues are initially delivered in order of attention accorded to them only; a setting allows them to be streamed alphabetically as well. Under each of the issues is a bar indicator of the origin of the issue—individual parties and the NGO basket. One may turn on and off individual parties and the NGO basket, allowing for comparison between two or more entities. This way one can note which entities share which issue terms. By turning off one or more issue-making entities, the issue stream refreshes itself, only showing the issues of the entities currently turned on. Loading in the center of the page are the issue attention graphs, in the style of stock price graphs. We have chosen a design frequently associated with currency or the moment—word streams with graphs showing currency over the past three months up to today.

Issue attention spreads have implications for each of the actors: the political parties, the press, and the NGOs. Especially for the political parties and the NGOs, one may understand and act upon issues depending on relative interest or relative disinterest. For example, issues may resonate only with a political party (and not to the press or to the NGOs); other issues may be relevant to NGOs and the press, but not to a political party. Yet another issue may resonate with political parties and the press, but not with NGOs. (We discuss some of the actions each of the groups may take with empirical data below.) For the press, any issue of a political party or an NGO (or especially a party-NGO issue) that does not resonate prompts reflection of why an issue is covered.

Here it is important to point out why we have not followed a kind of methodological symmetry and divined election issues from the press, then checked them against the parties and the NGOs. We dub an issue a press issue if it is an NGO or party issue with levels of press attention accorded to it. Crucially, we have not made the press into an independent source of issues, in order to monitor resonance of purely press issues at political party and NGO headquarters. This is a somewhat tricky point, for it is hardly defensible to argue that the press only covers, and does not make, issues, even if that may be a part of a journalistic ethos. Indeed, in chapter three (on food safety) we noted how the press (as well as the TV broadcasting company) seemingly attempted to make food safety an issue and staged a kind of debate through statement juxtaposition. It even glued together a (weak) network with actors linking to the story for a brief period of time.

Their lack of success in leading us to the debate (not to mention their attention span vis-à-vis other issue-makers) constitutes our overall concern in taking the press as independent issue source. If we were to evaluate issue-ness on the basis of network properties, we would allow the press sources to lead us to networks (if they do), and check issue-ness that way. Here, however, we are evaluating issue-ness according to currency. In undertaking this exercise, we would like to have the press retain its old-fashioned role—issue-currency-makers through coverage of others' issues. We would like them to provide us with clues about what the issues of currency may be, not what they are in advance of analysis.

Apart from the brief normative case for the press to play its old-fashioned role and keep to its ethos of covering, not making, issues, there are other important admissions we would like to make before turning to the analytical reason for keeping the press in its place. We have our practical reasons for not divining issues from the press. It is a principle of ours never to provide research feasibility arguments in defense of the direction of our proceedings. It is a great challenge, however, to analyze large collections of press articles through textual as well as content analysis, divining issue lists from them and subsequently comparing them to the parties' and to the NGOs'. We are unaware of research (methods, apparatus, tools, etc.) capable of accomplishing this feat adequately with this medium.[7] (At the time of writing, Google News had thirty days of news items available, where we are able now to make queries of the kind mentioned above.) To undertake this research ourselves we would have to capture certain full newspapers on a daily basis, for once the day has passed and the newspapers are digitally archived, complete editions are not available on the Web. The researcher can search archives by key words and receive individual articles, counts, headlines, and teaser texts. Indeed, as online versions of newspapers around the world continue to take up the *New York Times* format (of making available only today's and sometimes yesterday's full text, charging for the rest, and putting a cap on the number of articles one can access per month), we are being forced to build daily-capturing systems. There is a similar situation with capturing the TV news and (in a separate exercise) charting issue currency across the different media. To do it, one would make use of the subtitles and teletext of the TV news (for the hearing-impaired and for other challenging situations as loud cafés). There, too, we would have to capture daily, though archive innovation is somewhat more fluid than I describe, and opportunities often arrive suddenly, as with RSS technology.

There is, however, a much more important reason to allow the press to retain its conventional role. The political research we are pursuing in this instrumentation concerns issue currency trends in relation to NGO and political party agendas, and eventually we may be able to draw into relief much larger questions of whether (and when) the press drives politics.

There are many types of issue attention spans and scenarios that are of particular interest. We name some of the more significant ones based on the research initially undertaken some five months prior to the Dutch national elections of May 2002. These findings led us to believe that the system would be of some interest. Where the implications of attention spans are concerned, for example, one notes a steep decline in attention to a party issue (and for political personality researchers, to a party leader)—"Melkert-banen" (figure 5.2). Melkert was the candidate fielded by the Dutch Labour Party, and as the individual at the top of the party's list, would become the Prime Minister were the Labour Party victorious. One notes a sharp rise in attention to an issue identified by the NGOs only—"waiting lists" (figure 5.3). After a brief spike in attention accorded to an issue (around a summit), there is a precipitous fall

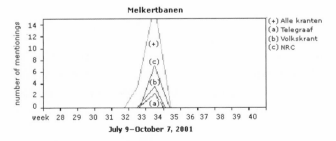

**Figure 5.2**
Attention spike to "Melkert-banen," an employment issue of the Labour Party, connected to the Labour Party leader and candidate for Prime Minister, Ad Melkert. Modified MS-Excel graph.

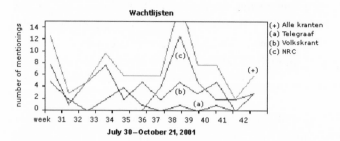

**Figure 5.3**
Continual attention accorded to a non-issue, waiting lists in health care. Modified MS-Excel graph.

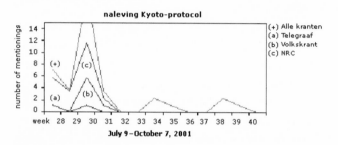

**Figure 5.4**
Attention decline to Labour Party issue (compliance with the Kyoto Protocol) after the Bonn summit. Modified MS-Excel graph.

in attention—"Kyoto Protocol" (figure 5.4). There are party issues that have no resonance—"European constitution" (figure 5.5), a different kind of non-issue. There are issues shared by parties and NGOs without press attention—"xeno-transplantation" (figure 5.6).

Where the implications of scenarios are concerned (for example, a sudden issue spike), events also may overtake political agendas carefully laid by parties and NGOs. Press attention (for example, to food safety and genetic manipulation) may spur the government to organize public debates including social groups allegedly already involved in a debate. NGOs may leave that debate, and lead us to another one that may tell us more.

Note the lack of press attention to the non-issue of genetic manipulation in figure 5.7. Is this to be read as a factor in the decision to stage a

**Figure 5.5**
No attention accorded to European Constitution, a Labour Party issue.
Modified MS-Excel graph.

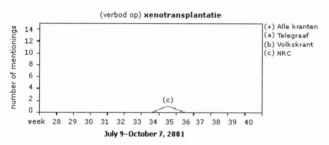

**Figure 5.6**
Low attention accorded to xeno-transplantation, an issue shared by the Labour
Party and the NGOs. Modified MS-Excel graph.

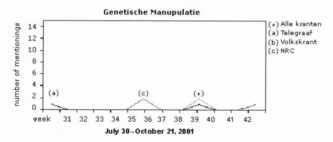

**Figure 5.7**
Mild attention to genetic manipulation, a non-issue and subject of *Eten en
Genen*, the government-organized public debate on GM food in 2001. Modified
MS-Excel graph.

public debate on GM food? Reading and interpreting press attention in relation to staged or unstaged agenda-setting, along the lines sketched above, is likely to be the task of the info-political strategist.[8]

But the virtue of the system so far conceived lies in its stinginess. It does not allow issues that are not part of party or NGO campaigns to appear until they become such. That is, there are no bolt-from-the-blue issues lurking in the system, but only those issues on the campaign agendas of the NGOs and the parties. This system stinginess allows us to approach (gradually) the larger issue; that is, the extent to which press drives politics. For example, we could approach ways of coming to grips, empirically, with a press event—that dreaded term one hears in disparagement of political stunts. Is a press event around a social issue one that only appears in the press (and not on the agendas of parties and NGOs)? The system would ignore that. Is a press event an issue statement juxtaposition that resonates in the press, and is picked up by certain parties and NGOs? Once picked up by parties and/or NGOs the system looks back (up to three months) to see how long it has taken for entities to attach themselves to the issue. Thus here it would display if a party or NGO is only reacting to press attention, or whether the issue has been under question by either for some time before. Will the party or the NGO measure itself by the extent to which it responds to the spike in press attention? When may it feel that it sullies itself in doing so? Will the party or NGO continue to stand on principle for themes that are not press-friendly? For how long would it do so? Thus, the system, as we have discussed in the introduction, has been designed first to ascertain press attention and subsequently to monitor how parties and social groups deal with dilemmas arising from attention. We put some of the dilemmas of the limelight on display and invite all to grapple not only with attention itself but also the monitoring of attention. Thus our instrument captures, and subsequently takes up, questions of the politics of attention.

**Tracker in Action: "Media helped Populism?"[9]**

On May 6, 2002, nine days prior to the Dutch national elections, Pim Fortuyn was shot dead in the Hilversum Media Park complex after giving a radio interview. Researchers and I were in Budapest at the time, holding

**Figure 5.8**
Pim Fortuyn graphic on the Pim Fortuyn Party Web site, January 2003. Source:
http://www.lijstpimfortuyn.nl/partij/images/silopim.jpg.

a workshop on the social life of issues and presenting the new Election
Issue Tracker finally on line at a Dutch political portal, politiek-
digitaal.nl. We had been watching how Pim Fortuyn's party issues were
climbing in press resonance, by virtue of a new system feature ranking
political parties according to the relative press attention each was receiving for its issues. Fortuyn's current party, Lijst Pim Fortuyn, and his previous party, Leefbar Nederland, were at the top of the rankings. Their
issues were being covered the most relative to the other parties' and
relative to all issue coverage.

But everything changed, for all parties ceased campaigning on May 7,
out of respect. Professor Pim, with his signature "at your service" salute,
was gone (see figures 5.8 and 5.9). The Prime Minister, Wim Kok,
declared himself *kapot*, expressing the tragedy as also one for the democracy and the rule of law. Thousands brought flowers and letters to
Fortuyn's doorstep in Rotterdam.[10] A few commentators expressed that,
whatever the consequences, the Netherlands might have lost a future
Prime Minister.

Despite mourning and concerns about overly emotive elections, the elections were held as scheduled on May 15, 2002. Lijst Pim Fortuyn registered the highest percentage rise in seats won of all parties, gaining 26 of
150 and a place in the ruling right-of-center coalition with the Christian
Democrats (CDA) and the Liberals (VVD). The Labour party (PvdA),
at the bottom of the list of the "press-friendliest parties" (according to

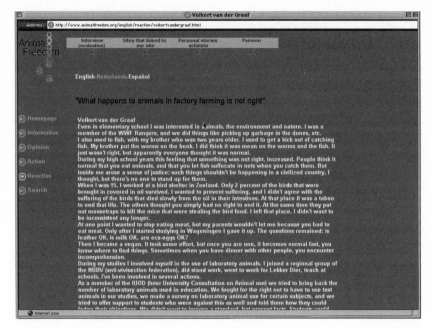

**Figure 5.9**
A "personal story" by Pim Fortuyn's assassin, Volkert van de Graaf, written in January 2002. The Web site was captured on May 8, 2002 and is no longer on its host, animalfreedom.org. A re-framed version appears at http://www.animalrights.net/articles/2002/000159.html, accessed on November 25, 2003.

our issue-resonance measure), witnessed the steepest decline in percentage of seats won.

We had not been interested in whether there was any measure of predictive value in the tracker or under which conditions it may have predictive value—a temptation in much analysis of this kind.[11] Such talk we found spurious, for there were too many other variables at work. Rather we desired to present a politics of attention and pose dilemmas for parties who may or may not have been witnessing press attention to their issues. Would they continue to stand, on principle, for issues not at all or barely resonating in the press? Would they abandon those issues, and pursue the issues towards the top of the rankings? Could we show when our defined informational politics—that is, parties taking up press-friendlier issues—were or were not on the rise, by whom and when? What would be the implications of these findings in terms of how we may wish to perform information politics with the Web? Would we wish to expose informational politics (with the Web)? Would we merely wish to add a stream of non-issues (the compilation of those NGO issues that have not as yet found a place on the parties' platforms), and thereby bring about another form of civil society issue politics in competition with political parties'?

In-fighting eventually would cause the Lijst Pim Fortuyn party to fall apart, resulting in new national elections in January 2003. Lijst Pim Fortuyn lost 18 seats (from its previous total of 26), symbolically putting an end to the Fortuyn phenomenon.

The new elections in 2003 have allowed us to approach the questions of whether and how the political parties are undertaking a form of informational politics, which we now may frame in terms of the uptake of populist issues by the other parties. At the outset, therefore, we shall not problematize the widespread branding of Pim Fortuyn's party as populist, but rather take it to be the case. We use his collection for the purposes of comparing relative Dutch party uptake of Fortuyn-populist issues between the 2002 and 2003 elections. We call our work an analysis of a form of informational politics for the populist issues that resonated most in the press in the run-up to the 2002 elections. There are two further moves to make in the argument. The first is that we will take populism to be a particular collection of issues. The second is to define those issues as having been taken up by Lijst Pim Fortuyn's party in the 2002 elections, relative to the overall set of issues by all parties. Thus with this heuristic we are able to classify the relative, shifting populism of parties by charting each party's relative uptake of populist issues. That is, which issues are Fortuyn's only, and which are only relatively Fortuyn's? Which parties would score highest now in a kind of populism metric that may be constructed on the basis of Fortuyn's issue list, the other parties' issue lists, and the changes between the other parties' issue lists between the elections? We also would like to know how well the parties that have taken on the most of his issues have done, absolutely as well as relative to their previous showing.

Before presenting the results of the analysis, one political system design decision—on the front-end—should be discussed (see figure 5.10). As mentioned above in passing, the Election Issue Tracker, as it was finally built, ranks issues as well as parties according to press-friendliness, a

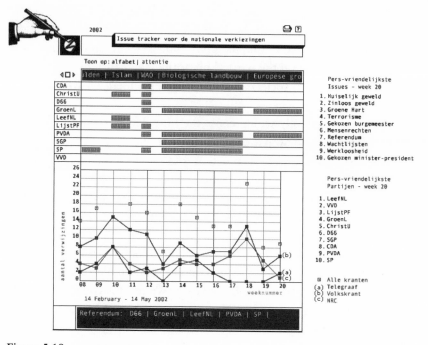

**Figure 5.10**
Election Issue Tracker, captured on election day, May 15, 2002, with populist
parties at the top of the week's press-friendliest rankings by virtue of their issues
resonating most in the press. Design by Anderemedia.nl and the Govcom.org
Foundation, programming by Recognos.ro, hosting by Politiek-digitaal.nl, and
party platform data collection for the 2002 and 2003 national elections by Jorie
Horsthuis and Steffie Verstappen.

term that may offend those who may feel there is no such thing or that
it should not be highlighted as such.[12] I am not able to resolve the larger
issue of the extent to which the press is predominantly following events
in the wild or following official statements, press releases, and other cans
made for press consumption. This is only accomplished in narrowed
undertakings (as our Genoa example), normally case by illustrative case,
though some larger scale work has been done.[13] But I would like to point
out that the government and political parties often employ sophisticated
press penetration as well as monitoring tools and act upon the findings.[14]
By dubbing issues press-friendly or less so, we are positioning the instrument within known tool-making as well as info-political practice, and
(again) using terms that are as literal as possible to politicize that prac-

tice. The aim is to politicize informational politics in two ways. First, we desire to present, brutally even, a tool for the informational politician, in the sense of a press-informational issue-politician. To a degree we are also building on top of what Castells calls "the crisis of credibility of the political system."

Captured into the media arena, reduced to personalised leadership, dependent on technologically sophisticated manipulation, pushed into unlawful financing, driven by and toward scandal politics, the party system has lost its appeal and trustworthiness, and, for all practical purposes, is a bureaucratic remainder deprived of public confidence.[15]

But, secondly, our applied informational politics have a normative edge for they are based on issue-friendliness in the press rather than personal and party friendliness. In other words, we are not measuring personality or party favorability by counting mentions and coding them, an analytical practice on the rise in our particular context in the Netherlands, justified by the Americanization of elections. It also normatively accepts popularity contests. We have chosen to distance our work from such undertakings for the normative issues discussed previously. (We would like elections to be about issues, and we would like to know whose issues the elections are about, from a press coverage standpoint). We also have distanced ourselves from the more typical and important analysis of whether or not voters are casting ballots on the basis of knowledge about which parties (or candidates) stand for which issues and if a lack of knowledge can be attributed to press coverage. This work, also about informational politics, is widespread, important, and often damning when we learn that, for example, people know more about the names of candidates' pets than their stands.[16] Our work, rather, concerns another relationship that is rather understudied; that is, whether political party issue selection moves in concert with press attention to issues.

We also have been interested in which issues are holding sway in our info-political arena as we have defined it. To us, informational politics concerns the increasing alignment between the issues the parties campaign for and the issues the press covers. In the Dutch case, are they Fortuyn's issues? Thus, the most important question in the follow-up to 2003 is, which populist issues are increasingly whose?

Finally, we continue to pursue the question of the persistence of populism being aided by the press. This becomes the trickiest inquiry, for if all or many parties reposition themselves in Fortuyn's issue space, then the extent to which the press is implicated in the rise of populism becomes more difficult to disentangle from the outcomes of its traditional role.

Of the ten leading political parties, six (including Fortuyn's) amended their platforms in December and early January 2003, just prior to the elections.[17] In 2003 we found that certain establishment parties—those doing most poorly in relative terms in the 2002 elections—had moved into the populist issue space that Pim Fortuyn's party and his previous party had occupied. We also found that Pim Fortuyn's party itself had left that issue terrain in 2003, moving into a distinct space not occupied by the other parties. Intriguingly, the populist issues (Pim Fortuyn's list and his former list) again received the most press resonance in 2003, further pointing to the press participation thesis, but the election results went against those parties.

Generally speaking, we have a situation from 2002 to 2003 whereby the establishment parties were moving in concert with populist issues, picking up the 2002 populist issues in their 2003 platforms. In 2002 and 2003 newspapers were wholly in step with populist issues; indeed, ahead of the establishment parties' uptake of those issues. (Figures 5.11 and 5.12 depict the relationships between parties and issues, using the analytical and visualization software RéseauLu, developed by Andrei Mogoutov of Aguidel, Paris. They show the relative movement of parties into the populist issue terrain around Lijst Pim Fortuyn, providing a comparison between the issue spaces the parties occupy in 2002 and 2003.)

We have taken the step of defining a particular form of informational politics and showing it in action across two national elections. Our undertaking has not been concerned with making a contribution to elections analysis—however much we have been tempted to do so—owing to the rapid succession of elections, the operation of the press monitoring tool throughout, the issue-party data sets collected, and the availability of sophisticated visualization software that shows parties clustering around issues. Indeed, we do not wish to lose sight of the larger goal of putting forward a practice of information politics with the Web.

At the outset we were looking to put the Web to use in order to complicate informational politics, initially by using the Web to capture non-issues. Subsequently, we have attempted to make a case for an instrument

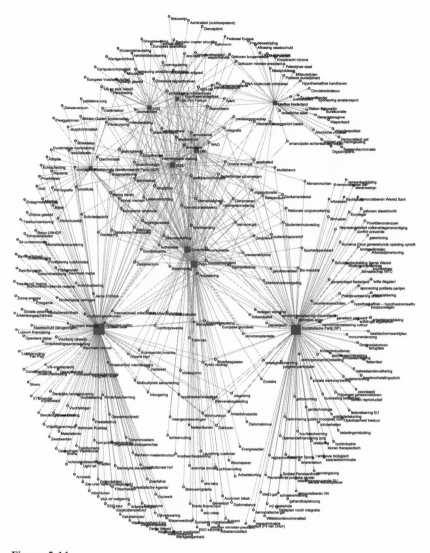

**Figure 5.11**
Dutch political parties clustering around issues, 2002. Visualization with RéseauLu by Andrei Mogoutov, Aguidel.com, and Marieke van Dijk.

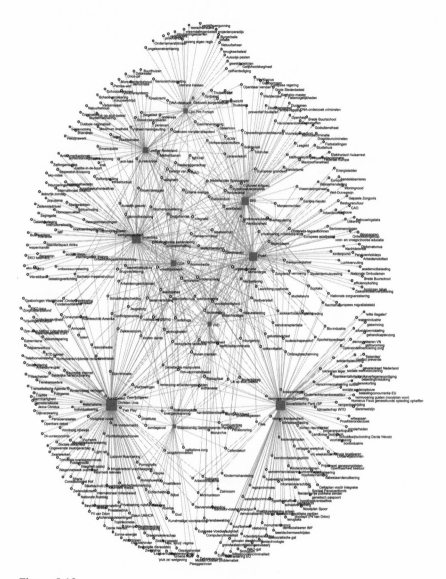

**Figure 5.12**
Dutch political parties clustering around issues, 2003. Visualization with
RéseauLu by Andrei Mogoutov, Aguidel.com, and Marieke van Dijk.

that would raise dilemmas for political parties with regard to how they handle press attention to issues. We did so in a timely fashion, when informational politics were also populist politics, in the terms defined above. As we have shown, parties moving in concert with the press-friendliest (populist) issues are called upon to perform their own searching info-political critiques, which, with the findings, have become particularly urgent.

Whilst not built into the final instrument, nonetheless we have proposed in our heuristic a symmetry of dilemmas, for civil society as well as for political parties. An invitation has been extended to the carriers of issues and non-issues to engage anew in a politics of press attention, the results of which we have put on display. Crucially, it is precisely that engagement—the concerted movement of issue-carriers and issue coverage—that is being monitored. The dilemmas remain.

## Appendixes

### Appendix 5.1   Web Issue Index of Civil Society, Echte Welvaart, October 2001 Stream

| Issues | # NGOs |
| --- | --- |
| 1. Duurzaamheid | 8 |
| 2. Milieu | 7 |
| 3. Natuur | 4 |
| 4. Gezondheidszorg | 4 |
| 5. Dierenwelzijn | 3 |
| 6. Agrariërs | 3 |
| 7. Biologische diversiteit | 2 |
| 8. Biologisch voedsel | 2 |
| 9. Genetische manipulatie | 2 |
| 10. Medezeggenschap | 2 |
| 11. Non-vaccinatiebeleid | 2 |
| 12. Onderwijs | 2 |
| 13. Behoud open ruimte | 2 |
| 14. Vrijwilligerswerk | 2 |
| 15. Verantwoordelijkheid | 2 |
| 16. Wachtlijsten (zorg) | 2 |

| | |
|---|---|
| 17. Xenotransplantatie | 2 |
| 18. Afvalscheiding | 2 |
| 19. Armoede | 2 |
| 20. Derde wereld | 2 |
| 21. Gelijkwaardigheid | 2 |
| 22. Keuzevrijheid (zorg) | 2 |
| 23. Groene energie | 2 |

# NGOs = Number of organizations doing the issue.

**Appendix 5.2    Party-NGO Issues and NGO Issues only (Non-issues)**

| Party-NGO Issues | Non-issues |
|---|---|
| 1. Vrijwilligerswerk | 1. Milieu |
| 2. Xenontransplantatie | 2. Natuur |
| 3. Groene energie | 3. Dierenwelzijn |
| 4. Biologische diversiteit | 4. Agrariërs |
| 5. Duurzaamheid | 5. Genetische manipulatie |
| 6. Armoede | 6. Medezeggenschap |
| 7. Gezondheidszorg | 7. Non vaccinatiebeleid |
| | 8. Behoud open ruimte |
| | 9. Verantwoordelijkheid |
| | 10. Keuzevrijheid (zorg) |
| | 11. Gelijkwaardigheid |
| | 12. Derde wereld |
| | 13. Biologisch voedsel |
| | 14. Wachtlijsten (zorg) |
| | 15. Afvalscheiding |
| | 16. Onderwijs (not graphed) |
| The PvdA (Labour Party) and the Echte Welvaart have the above issues in common. | The Echte Welvaart issues not shared by the PvdA (Labour Party). |

# 6

# The Practice of Information Politics on the Web

I would like to summarize the arguments made in this book that lead to new forms of information politics with the Web. At the outset we have attempted to build a foundation for a Web epistemological practice that takes seriously information embedded in the medium, especially information that captures Web dynamics and can be analyzed for the purposes of the adjudication of sources. Much of the defense has concerned how to make use of the Web through this theorized practice. It has argued for the value of this approach in terms of how the Web may sustain itself as a space that displays the collision of different accounts of reality—realities that may compete well with those they challenge, as argued directly in the Viagra, food safety and Genoa cases.[1] We have been positioning the information instruments discussed in the book as following a particular epistemological practice as well as leading to an information politics with the Web. These are information politics that challenge both classic politics—the citizen-government exchanges, public debates—and informational politics—the highly mediated versioning of reality in the news and elsewhere that is aligned with official communication strategies.

In critiquing current Web practices and the informational politics they lead to, we also have shown how current back-end and front-end politics may provide the framework for doing classic politics as well as informational politics, with disappointing results. In the front-end political cases of the UK online Citizens' Portal and the Dutch public debate organized by the government, we have witnessed what Castells and others have called the "crisis of democracy," defining it in part as a problem of editing out social debate. In the UK case, there is the pre-formatting of the debate to fit ministerial responsibilities and the blocking of inputs outside the governmental debate space as well as the continual removal of postings. In the Dutch case there is the disregard for actors from the leading international standard-setting forums (Codex, WTO) and the winnowing of the terms of debate that prompted the departure of the leading Dutch NGOs. In both cases, the results are disappointing in the obvious sense that the government must admit the failure of classic politics (owing to its editing practices and its formats), but more importantly in the sense that the crisis only continues.

On the back-end we have discussed how certain logics and practices are taking the Web away from its public-spiritedness. The dominant search engine logics are beginning to lead to a system of information exposure not in keeping with the principle of scope of representation. An argument may be made that there are serious consequences in engines having finally solved the correspondence problem between queries and returns (also called the resolution of the real name issue). For example, a query for GATT these days returns in the dominant engines the WTO and sites pointing to it and no longer returns the parody site gatt.org in their higher rankings. One also cannot directly ask the engine how highly gatt.org is ranked. Thus the engine also does not display the extent to which its back-end politics are in alignment with informational politics. In solving the correspondence problem, the dominant engine logics have at the same time edited out side-by-sideness. The engine-based medium, if we may see the Web as such for a moment, thereby un-flattens sources, leading in particular to the emergence of more familiar (front-end) hier- archies of credibility at the expense of scope of representation and expo- sure to a range of arguments.

These we have put forward as illustrative cases of information poli- tics: back-ends and front-ends doing informational politics well or doing classic politics badly. In all cases, we witness the re-authoring of the crisis of democracy in the new medium. The crisis is re-enacted time and again when the imported government-organized debate format fails to account convincingly for the ongoing social debate.

To make the general argument, we have striven to sort the cases in an elementary framework (back-end and front-end politics aligning with informational politics or classic politics), clarifying what a debate about information politics and the Web may be about.[2] We do this also to engage from the sidelines in the e-democracy debate, where attempts are made to execute classic politics with the Web. Far and wide, governments are designing sites for citizen input—the e-democracy experiments of which the UK online Citizens' Portal is the tip of the iceberg. We are not so naïve as to believe that these experiments designed to bring the citizen and the public into the process of agenda-setting and policy-making will go away with this book, or that the spirit to do so should go away. Indeed, the quest to locate valuable citizen contributions continues online, in the case of a proposal for a British spam filtering system that would edit out emails from lobbyists, leaving only genuine citizen input.[3] Though we argue for our approach in relation to the failings of such experimentation (and the levity of such an idea), we are not so bold-faced in our pronouncements for abandoning all experiments in this direction. Along these lines, our point would be that such experimentation, often high-profile, only briefly masks the crisis (whilst quietly re-enacting it).[4] The experimentation (which, like ours, is also a kind of practice) also does not tend to make the point that the Internet may be better suited for capturing the collision between the official and the less-official. It also does not argue that the Web may be better suited to point to the collision as a competition that may be staged as such.

The research behind this book has been undertaken in connection with the Dutch government initiative Infodrome. With the leeway provided by a governmental information society project, especially in a Dutch context, the work commenced in 2000 with the remarkable reference to the leftovers of an old public-spirited Internet. We took this to mean a medium once challenging the official through its new information politics and cultures—an Internet culture, stark in contrast to the new harsher protectionist cultures and closed spaces, with its practices and arguments currently deriving from the rise of information law.[5] From that contrasted public-spiritedness came our striving to make use of the ever-increasing medium information and ever-vibrant medium methods of adjudication, and set them up to challenge the disembedded anew.

We have begun by exploring certain adjudication techniques arriving from the medium culture that are themselves embedded. We have discussed the case of collaborative filtering more generally, as well as the particular arxiv.org model where scientific papers are ranked on the basis of freshness as well as on the basis of the references they receive only

from within the online archive—a particular mix of ranking not generally practiced in science.[6] The model, it turns out, has not transferred
well to other scientific arenas for reasons discussed earlier having to do
with perceptions of the trustworthiness of the medium adjudication cultures as well as classic sub-politics. We would like to see whether these
perceptions must continue to hold sway.

Broadly speaking, in setting out a course for defining how to revive a
public-spirited Internet and, at the same time, redo information politics
with the Web cultures, we first have attempted to define more precisely
the space in which we would like to situate our undertakings. Drawing
up the matrices and placing current Web projects as well as our information instruments in them (in the opening chapter) has been an effort
to organize culture, epistemology, and politics, or more precisely public-
spirited medium culture, Web epistemology, and information politics. We
are interested in a theorized practice that, to the greatest extent achiev-
able (on the back-ends and front-ends), allows us to sit atop the cultures
(instead of participating in them or asking them to participate in ours),
watch how they adjudicate (instead of imposing editorial order on them),
and show as well as interrogate the kinds of information politics that
result. This has been the overall thought behind the practice, our means
for renewal.

In reconciling our practice with certain public-spirited principles as
well as the adjudication methods of certain medium cultures, we have
had to take some positions and make some decisions. First we introduced
noble system design principles put forward by political analysts. We
understood them as a back-end practice as well as a means of evaluating front-end output. In putting forward public-spiritedness on both
ends, the political analysts were endeavoring to move the discussion
beyond mere disclosure of sub-politics—the deal-making that results in
obscuring paid inclusion and preferred placement in dominant engine
returns. In stepping beyond Ralph Nader and other's politics to ones that
take seriously inclusivity, scope of representation, and fairness on the
back ends and front ends, we took it upon ourselves to build with the
political analysts and make our next moves. Those systems that achieve
to some degree the political design principles enumerated above—for
example, open directory projects—have adjudication cultures that have
arisen with and been shaped by the Web. While suffering from the impo-

sition of principles on information cultures that do not practice them—the cases of commercial and e-democratic information come to mind—and subsequently editing some out, they do still provide clues as to the necessity of taking the combination of public-spiritedness and medium adjudication cultures seriously. On the front-end they also challenge informational politics by providing alternatives. In often editing out the commercial and the governmental, however, these cultures themselves do not live up to that longed-for public-spirited feature of the Web—side-by-sideness. This is the challenge—not to epistemologically privilege through particular editing practices (as well as other back-end politics). It is also the challenge, similar to the one put to Google above, to allow queries for that which is edited out. But such critiques made of the editors are both too easy as well as answerable, except, perhaps, when it is demonstrated that other approaches may address what we have dubbed the tyrannies of editors and the debates about them, in the style of *der Nörgler*—the complaining critic construct offered by Karl Kraus earlier this century. In parting company with voluntaristic culture (self-reporting), and instead opting for allowing the commercial, governmental, and non-governmental parties to carry on as usual without vetting and selective editing, we were beginning to take positions and make decisions. We are interested in ascertaining whether our approach to the sea of information—that is, to allow the evaluative mechanisms in place on the Web to dictate how information is captured and adjudicated—is able to withstand a searching info-political critique.

In developing what also may be called an info-political epistemology with the Web, we have striven to specify the heuristics of a particular Web practice (on the back-end) and a set of principles for the evaluation of the output on the front-end. These positions have resulted in the following elements that our practice and instruments attempt to achieve. First, we follow the principle of side-by-sideness through non-voluntaristic collection of sources. Second, blaming the Web (instead of editors), we use embedded information for our means of adjudication. In doing so, we still seek to achieve scope of representation, exposure to a range of arguments beyond the highly mediated, and social-ness, which are also our means of evaluating our own information politics on the front-end. We also desire to have results with a deeper ontology and (reflexively) open logics inviting what was once termed manipulation.

That depth is our contribution to the front-end Web. Open logics, showing how actors are reacting to the readings of the instruments, are our contribution to the back-end. The elements that we have had to abandon are fairness, inclusivity in adjudication with a voluntaristic collection method resulting in flat ontology and, in the case of engines and to a certain extent in the case of editors, in closed logics.

## Political Instrument Design

As we were beginning our instrument design with those principles in mind and with questions about the kind of information politics and, just as importantly, the kind of Web those principles may lead to in practice, there was still another step to make in connection with certain overall perceptions about the medium. Concerns about the quality of information on the Web live on, concerns that may be disentangled from the results of side-by-sideness—the eminent and the crackpot in the same list of authoritative returns.[7] We began with exercises that attempted to sweep away some of the hardened notions about Internet quality that drive projects to create trustworthy (edited, vetted) information, as with the initiative supported the Dutch Ministry of Health. In order to address information quality issues, we decided to take one of the most difficult cases—the under-regulated sex drug Viagra. Certainly here, one suspects, the Internet could show itself to be a tawdry medium in need of a serious expert edit. With the aid of a non-voluntaristic adjudicating procedure, we took advantage of not the tawdry but the real, or what we dubbed the proximity of the Web, in certain cases to an underground and to a street culture. How would street culture fare next to the official sources? What would we learn from what we called the collision between official and unofficial accounts of reality? We found that the Web, in this new guise as collision space and reality checker, could become an anticipatory medium, one that identifies unrecognized users and unrecognized Viagra situations as rather normal. By providing the commercial and non-commercial keepings of our collaborative filterers with some demonstrable Web expertise, we would show that we are knowledgeable about what is going on beyond that presented by the medical industry and the governmental regulators (as well as the newspapers which sometimes reinstall the "Viagra as medicine only" story). Poke at 40 pounds, resellers with 10 percent commissions, women in abnormal and non-loving situations—normal realities are often underacknowledged in particular information practices. The Web, however, can be made to deepen and enrich the outcomes of a collision between the official and the unofficial. More specifically, we would show how usage and scenario information could make a difference for the officially unrecognized users and for the second and third parties in Viagra situations. Our information politics—exposing the real as well as calling forth new subjects and new situations—were derived from street awareness gleaned from the Web.

We were beginning to cross information streams, or analyze multiple sites according to a certain practice and to make arguments about how to conjure info-political spaces on the Web. The next step was to begin comparisons with traditional sources—the everyday default information and decision-making sources (the press, white papers, public debate programs) that are also doing informational politics and classic politics with and without the Web. Both in the Viagra case, but also mid-way into the issue barometer, we had begun to show how the Web may be used as a checking mechanism (to enrich and complicate official sources through a flattening of hierarchies of credibility—an information politics from below). To continue with that task, we had to position our Web techniques and our findings within known, competing contexts; that is, what is the difference between the story of food safety debate in the newspaper and from the public debate in buildings and the findings from the Web about what it is and where it may be taking place? Could we demonstrate how the Web may be employed to expose informational politics—to show the alignment of media stories of a debate about food safety with efforts to organize one by the government? Could the Web, more importantly, put on display the challenges ahead in ever trying to do classic politics without it?

In asking that question, we began to arrive at new uses for the medium. Perhaps the Web may be used not only as an anticipatory but also as an explanatory medium, in this case for public disinterest in food safety, and also for the failure of classic politics—the public debate format in the Netherlands where genuine citizens, established actors, and the government come together to arrive at a consensus (or dissensus) on policy. First, exposure was undertaken. Government may know that the food safety debate is going on elsewhere. We found this by analyzing the White Paper and pointing to the obligation of any debate passing through the Codex Alimentarius Commission, WTO, and EU. We thought, however, that the government may be masking knowledge of the international passage points in its attempts at doing classic politics by gathering the usual national subjects and organizing a public debate without the key international players. Many key national actors (15 leading NGOs) also left the debate, as we have aimed to show, with precisely that knowledge. Second, and more importantly, we tried to remind ourselves (and demonstrate with the Web) that in fact those actors were not so much leaving the debate as returning to it. In taking some pains and various detours in order to have the Web and the Web techniques locate the debate, we gradually came to the more difficult idea that the Web could be a primary source for understanding the conditions of failed classic politics. Perhaps, too, it could lead to another kind of politics— an issue network politics, embryonic forms of which we could witness in counter-summits that could in future follow a practice of participant adjudication along Web-epistemological lines. This would be the virtual roundtable construct. At the very least, if classic politics must be done, in the old spirit or in its various reincarnations in e-democracy, we showed that one may as well check where the debate is before attempting the challenging exercise of relocating and re-territorializing it. Thus our instrument engages with the e-democracy debate, providing a very different road ahead.

In approaching the Web as primary source (and in eventually providing it in the Web Issue Index), there were great hurdles to clear. "What news from Genoa?" Shylock asked in *The Merchant of Venice*. The news is not good, we may have read, and neither is the coverage. Instead of arguing from the point of view of critical press analysts and deconstructing the (legitimate or illegitimate) communication strategies that drive coverage (proving informational politics once more), we attempted at least to confirm ideas about poor coverage, and then defend a new stream of civil society aims that could provide a remedy. We had to contextualize the new stream, for there are many, as at Oneworld and Indymedia. The defense of the particular stream put forward rested on the relative stability of issue definitions; that is, we need not compete with the press in the informational political arena (as Oneworld and Indy-media do) and deliver news everyday about issues, supplementing the record. The issues are more stable, though civil society attention to them rises and falls. We thought that awareness of the stability of issues was important in itself—the good news from Genoa—but we took the further step of showing whether and when the issues are waxing or waning, so action may be taken, also from the issue's point of view.

In chapter four we did not mention why we colored declining issues red. One may believe that the more an issue is being treated in cam-paigns, the hotter (more red) it becomes. The instrument, however, takes the position of the issue itself—warning, in some sense, that it is not being cared for. Here we reformulate and make more real what pre-viously may have appeared ludicrous—caring for and nurturing the artificial. Crucially, we are striving to make use of a kind of living Web (embedded information together with the adjudication that it provides), but we are also endeavoring to allow for another outcome—one quite distinct from the device achievements resulting in coffee machines being shown on Web cams or gardens being tended remotely, and quite dis-tinct from the information achievements resulting in Britney Spears topping the list of all engine queries made this week, however significant or intriguing they may be. Information about the life of the issue becomes a means to see whether it is decision time for civil society. We argued, more significantly, that issuefication, or the means by which an issue is turned into a collective cause for concern and action, may have other sources, sources different from press attention to issues and different from shifts in inter-governmental agendas (for example, the call for more volunteering by the UN, and making that call "the year of," a subject treated in chapter three). While we found that issues are more stable than the press attention granted to them, we also attempted to create a means to make another kind of call, one beyond calendar work. The red issue is in decline, not in the UN or the press, but in civil society. Thus we are practicing an issue information politics with civil society.

In making this move, we thus started to enter into the dynamics, dependencies, and consequences of attention, first in the case of NGO campaigns and then, ultimately, in that of political parties' standing for issues, especially in the run-up to elections. While the Web may still be used as anticipatory and explanatory medium with this stream, here it begins to take on kind of a soul-searching role.

The dilemmas of press attention were the subject of our final instrument. The Election Issue Tracker, initially, builds on top of the Web Issue Index. The civil society issue stream is compared to parties' streams captured from their online political platforms. Which issues do they have in common; which issues are only those of civil society? In dubbing those civil society themes not on the party platforms non-issues we are again in the info-political arena. But the more significant moves are the next ones. We are interested in the competition between issues for attention, the non-issues, and the party issues. Since we had provided an information politics with civil society in the Web Issue Index, we did not concentrate our efforts on showing whether civil society issues wax or wane with press attention. (They appeared not to in the Genoa case, albeit in a different national media context, in only an illustrative case.) Rather, we desired to do information politics with political parties. We concerned ourselves with relationships between press attention and party attention to issues, as well as the larger question of relationships between informational politics and issue politics.

With the Web Issue Index, issue politics had been defined as the extent to which the state of the issue (its redness) would drive renewed campaign attention. The Web Issue Index provides a demonstrable issue urgency measure distinct from others derived, for example, from intergovernmental agendas or press attention. With the Election Issue Tracker, we are now allowed to see whether political parties are principled issue-keepers. We ask which matter most, the press-friendliest issues or the party-principled issues? The results disappoint.

In building the Election Issue Tracker, we desired to display with the Web the competition between informational politics and issue politics— another level of the reality collision principle we have been following. In the narrative we have spent some time expressing our gratitude to the newspapers for their public-spiritedness in allowing unfettered access to full-text archives (and also not double-counting issue mentions in single articles). At the time of writing, however, the newspapers here are beginning to take up the model where one may query and receive article counts per issue (and a few opening lines of each article), but may not verify the reliability of their archive returns through a full-text analysis.

(*De Telegraaf* is the exception.) In consequence, this is akin to closed logics, but that is not the issue here. At issue, rather, is what the press is covering, and whether parties' issue selections are in step with the issues that resonate the most. With the rise of populism, in the guise of the popularity of Pim Fortuyn and his standing for a particular collection of issues widely branded as such, the stakes are particularly great.

In 2002 and early 2003 we queried three leading newspapers daily and watched how political party issues rose and fell in a system that ranked parties according to the relative coverage of each party's issues (and also relative to coverage of all issues). This is an issue impact measure. We found in 2002 that Pim Fortuyn's and other populist issues resonated the most in the press. With this finding in hand, we cautiously put forward the heretical claim that the press participated in the rise of populism. In 2003 the populist issues also were covered the most, though the populist parties did poorly in the elections. Finally, we witnessed how the establishment parties that had a poor showing in the previous elections moved into the populist issue space, perhaps providing an indication of why the populist parties fared less well in 2003.

In chapter five we put forward these blunt and sobering findings, pointing up the normality of informational politics (as we have defined it), but also perhaps providing indications of the rationale behind civil society press penetration strategies, a subject of chapter four. There we put forward that one of the greater paradoxes, even tragedies, of civil society these days is a continued reliance on measuring the value of their activities by press appearance. Despite the rise of independent and Internet forms of news as well as the great importance placed by analysts and by civil society on networks and networking, many NGOs still rely on commercial press coverage as demonstrable evidence of worth.[8] Indeed, the sophistication of an NGO is often thought of in terms of its press communication strategy (for example, Greenpeace).

At the same time, reliance on the press and a media strategy may raise questions about integrity and authenticity. A case in point—the political parties shamelessly moved into the populist issue space. The political parties thereby resolved their dilemma of standing for issues in principle or moving in concert with press-friendly issues, largely by adding the populist issues to their platforms. Civil society, however, may not have the luxury of resolving the dilemma so effortlessly.

For civil society the urgent question becomes the extent to which their work may *not* be driven by coverage. Similarly, and related to the question of coverage, is another potential impact of the news on NGOs. When do NGOs take up issues that do not depend on the press coverage of the same issues? In asking about the extent to which NGOs are not beholden to the press in terms of self-worth and issue-worth, as well as issue selection, we also would like to know if the Web and, particularly, network politics can make a difference. We would like to know whether attunement to informational politics must continue, or whether new forms of information politics may be accomplished.

In chapter three we plotted issue networks to ascertain whether emergent forms of politics are taking place beyond the classic national citizen-government exchanges as well as beyond the intergovernmental agenda-setting framework. We did so in an effort to explain the failure of classic politics. Now we are asking questions, in conclusion, about the extent to which issue network politics may challenge informational politics.

For an NGO one may ask whether coverage of itself or of its issues is significantly related to its standing in its network. The networks may have other means of distributing standing and other ways of choosing as well as persisting with issues. Indeed, we may find that NGO standing, issue-making, and issue-keeping have little to do with the leanings of the press. Moreover, they may have less to do with the agendas of governmental and inter-governmental organizations. Indeed, they may be putting forth worthy competition. We have found this for Genoa, in reporting the good news about issue stability from Italy. Recall that the dedicated civil society stream was defended because of its distinctiveness vis-à-vis particular inter-governmental agendas, upholding civil society's distance from the state.

With informational politics becoming the norm and with classic politics in tatters, the extent to which other forms of politics may challenge the two becomes crucial. Whilst the questions remain central, they are asked in reaction to the provision of a series of instruments that expose blunt informational politics on the one hand and put forward potentially competing and unsettling issue network politics, issue politics, and a politics from below, on the other. This is how we would like to summarize our series.

Finally, we have argued that the Web may be the primary platform where civil society issues are displayed. As such it is also one of the few places where one may stage the encounter between issue (network) politics and informational politics. With the engines, the summits, the governmental sites, the public debates, and the news doing informational politics well and classic politics poorly, the Web has a new purpose. Whilst often thought of as benefitting civil society, the Web, brought to life through a particular practice, may very well be for the public, too.

# Notes

## Chapter 1

1. I use "we" as a shorthand reference to "researchers and I." For a list of the researchers and their contributions, please see the Preface.

2. Richard Grusin, "Pre-mediation," *Criticism* (forthcoming).

3. Cf. previous search engine tampering practices discussed in Richard Rogers, "Introduction: Towards the Practice of Web Epistemology," in *Preferred Placement: Knowledge Politics on the Web*, ed. Richard Rogers. Maastricht: Jan van Eyck Editions, 2000: 11–23.

4. Google, as well as most every other engine, allows "self-reporting" in the form of URL submissions, but Google does not allow the self-reporting to influence how the site or page is ranked or with which key words the site or page is associated. In this sense, its adjudicating practices are non-voluntaristic. See also http://www.google.com/addurl.html; and Tara Calishain and Rael Dornfest, *Google Hacks*. San Sebastopol, CA: O'Reilly, 2003.

5. Letter from U.S. Federal Trade Commission to search engine companies, June 27, 2002, http://www.ftc.gov/os/closings/staff/commercialalertattatch.htm, accessed on September 2, 2002.

6. Princeton Survey Research Associates, "A Matter of Trust: What Users Want from Websites," Princeton, NJ, January, 2002, at http://www.consumer Webwatch.com/news/report1.pdf, accessed on September 2, 2002.

7. Lucas Introna and Helen Nissenbaum, "The Public Good Vision of the Internet and the Politics of Search Engines," in *Preferred Placement*, 44.

8. http://www.commercialalert.org, accessed on November 18, 2002.

9. Letter from Consumer Alert to Mr. Donald Clark, Secretary, Federal Trade Commission, July 16, 2001, http://www.commercialalert.org/index.php?category_id=1&subcategory_id=24&article_id=33, accessed on September 2, 2002.

10. Steve Lawrence and C. Lee Giles, "Searching the Web," *Science* 280 (1999): 98–100; and Steve Lawrence and C. Lee Giles, "Accessibility of Information on the Web," *Nature* 400 (1999): 107–109. See also discussions in Alberto-László Barabási, *Linked: The New Science of Networks*. Cambridge, MA: Perseus,

2002: 161–178; and Bernardo Huberman, *The Laws of the Web: Patterns in the Ecology of Information*. Cambridge, MA: MIT Press, 2002.

11. See also Vincent Miller, "Search Engines, Portals and Global Capitalism," in *Web.Studies*, ed. David Gauntlett. New York: OUP, 2000, 113–121.

12. Lucas Introna and Helen Nissenbaum, "The Public Good Vision of the Internet," 46.

13. Manuel Castells, *The Power of Identity*. Oxford: Blackwell, 1997: 309–353.

14. Eben Moglen fills in disintermediation this way: "The Internet is actually a social condition where everyone in the network society is connected directly, without intermediation, to everyone else." Eben Moglen, "Anarchism Triumphant: Free Software and the Death of Copyright," *FirstMonday* 4, no. 8 (1999), http://www.firstmonday.org/issues/issue4_8/moglen.

15. Cass Sunstein, *Republic.com*. Princeton, N.J.: Princeton University Press, 2001: 33.

Nicholas Negroponte, *Being Digital*. New York: Alfred A. Knopf, 1995: 195.

16. http://www.google-watch.org, accessed on February 12, 2003.

17. Ulrich Beck, *Risikogesellschaft: Auf dem Weg in eine andere Moderne*. Frankfurt/M: Suhrkamp, 1986: 18.

18. http://www.ukonline.gov.uk/citizenspace/discussions, accessed on December 15, 2001.

19. On some of the elements of medium culture, and how they may conflict with traditional disciplinary approaches to studying culture, see Steve Jones, "Studying the Net: Intricacies and Issues," in *Doing Internet Research: Critical Issues and Methods for Examining the Net*, ed. Steve Jones. London: Sage, 1999: 17.

20. http://www.ukonline.gov.uk/about/terms.php, accessed on December 15, 2001.

21. P.E. Athanasekou, "Internet and Copyright: An Introduction to Caching, Linking and Framing," work in progress, *The Journal of Information, Law and Technology* 2 (1998), http://elj.warwick.ac.uk/jilt/wip/98_2atha.

22. Korinna Patelis, "E-mediation by America Online," in *Preferred Placement*, 49–63; and Jodi Dean, "Virtual Fears," *Signs: Journal of Women in Culture and Society* 24, no. 4 (1999): 1069–1078.

23. Noortje Marres and Gerard de Vries, *Tussen Toegang en Kwaliteit: Legitimatie en Contestatie van Expertise op het Internet*. Den Haag: Wetenschappelijke Raad voor het Regeringsbeleid, 2002.

24. http://www.gezondheidskiosk.nl, accessed on September 12, 2001.

25. "Pictures in our heads" is an expression used by Walter Lippmann, *Public Opinion*. New York: Free Press, 1997, 3–11.

26. See also Josh On's http://www.theyrule.net, accessed on October 10, 2001.

27. Noortje Marres, "Somewhere you've got to draw the line: De politiek van selectie op het Web," M.Sc. thesis, University of Amsterdam, 2000.

28. Karl Kraus, *Die letzen Tage der Menschheit*. Frankfurt/M: Suhrhamp, 1992.

29. The rejection by arxiv.org of papers submitted by individuals with a hotmail address comes from personal communication with Rob Kling during the Joint International conference of the European Association for the Study of Science and Technology (EASST) and the Society for the Social Study of Science (4S), Vienna, September 27–30, 2000.

30. Heath Bunting, http://www.irational.org/heath/, especially http://www. irational.org/heath/_readme.html, accessed on August 15, 2001.

31. http://dir.yahoo.com/Computers_and_Internet/Internet/Devices_Connected_ to_the_Internet, accessed on February 20, 2003.

32. Steve Jones, "Studying the Net," 6–7. See also http://www.visualroute.com.

33. For Webometrics see the work of the Networked Research and Digital Information (NERDI) group at the Royal Academy of Arts and Sciences, Netherlands Institute for Scientific Information, http://www.niwi.knaw.nl/nerdi, accessed on February 20, 2003.

34. Rob Kling, Joanna Fortuna, and Adam King, "The Real Stakes of Virtual Publishing: The Transformation of E-Biomed into PubMed Central," CIS working paper WP-01-03, SLIS, Indiana University, 2001, http://www.slis. indiana.edu/CSI/wp01-03.html.

35. Lev Manovich, *The Language of New Media*. Cambridge, MA: MIT Press, 2001, 8–10; and Nina Wakeford, "New Media, New Methodologies: Studying the Web," *Web.Studies*, 31–41.

36. Steve Jones, ed., *Encyclopedia of New Media*. Thousand Oaks, CA: Sage, 2003.

37. See also Jennifer Tann, Adrian Platts, Sarah Welch, and Judy Allen, "Patient Power? Medical Perspectives on the Patient Use of the Internet," *Prometheus* 21, no. 2 (2003): 145–160.

38. See also Pieter van Wesemael, *Architecture of Instruction and Delight: A Socio-Historical Analysis of the World Exhibition as a Didactic Phenomenon, 1798–1851–1970*. Rotterdam: 010 Publishers, 2001.

39. See discussion on testing the quality of house party drugs at http://www. ggdkennisnet.nl/kennisnet, accessed on October 10, 2001.

40. For the *Netlocator* as well as the *IssueCrawler* software and instructions of use, see http://www.govcom.org. The IssueCrawler is at http://issuecrawler.net.

## Chapter 2

1. An argument of this kind has been made in Richard Rogers and Noortje Marres, "French Farmers on the Streets and on the Web: Stretching the Limits of Reported Reality," *Asian Journal of Social Science* 30, no. 2 (2002): 339–353.

2. Martin Svoboda, the Director of the Czech Republic's State Technical Library, recalled reading Nick Arnett, "Mendicant Sysops in Cyberspace," *TidBITS* 225/09 (May 1994), http://www.tidbits.com/tb-issues/TidBITS-225.html,

accessed on November 28, 2003. I would like to thank Rima Kupryte, formerly of the Open Society Institute, Budapest, for the introduction.

3. Edward Fox, *The Hungarian Who Walked to Heaven: Alexander Csoma de Körös, 1784–1842*. London: Short Books, 2001. See also Alexander Csoma de Körös, *A Dictionary of Tibetan and English*. New Delhi: Cosmo, 1978; Alexander Csoma de Körös, *Grammar of the Tibetan Language*. Budapest: Akademiai Kiado, 1984; and Alexander Csoma de Körös, *Tibetan Studies*. Budapest: Akademiai Kiado, 1984. There is another Tibetan connection, for Viagra competes with certain Tibetan animal-based virility products.

4. Vannevar Bush, "As We May Think," *Atlantic Monthly* 176, no. 1 (July 1945): 101–108, at http://www.theatlantic.com/unbound/flashbks/computer/bushf.htm. See also James M. Nyce and Paul Kahn, eds. *From Memex to Hypertext: Vannevar Bush and the Mind's Machine*. New York: Academic Press, 1991; and Paul Resnick and Hal R. Varian, "Recommender Systems," *Communications of the ACM* 40, no. 3 (1997) 56, 58.

5. Anne Branscomb, *Who Owns Information? From Privacy to Public Access*. New York: Basic Books, 1995. For a thoughtful debate around trading privacy for product, see *Harper's* (January 2000): 57–68.

6. Maureen Dowd in the *New York Times*, reprinted in the *International Herald Tribune* (December 16, 2001).

7. Matthew Chalmers, "Cookies Are Not Enough: Tracking and Enriching Web Activity with a Recommender System," in *Preferred Placement*, 99–111. See also http://www.epinions.com.

8. See Tim Berners-Lee and Mark Fishcetti, *Weaving the Web: The Original Design and Ultimate Destiny of the World Wide Web by its Inventor*. San Francisco: HarperCollins, 1999; and J. Langer, "Physicists in the New Era of Electronic Publishing," *Physics Today Online* 53, no. 8 (August 2000): 35, http://www.aip.org/pt/vol-53/iss-8/p35.html.

9. James Glanz, "The Web as Dictator of Scientific Fashion," *New York Times* (June 19, 2001).

10. Arxiv.org. <http://www.arxiv.org.>

11. Pornography and piracy are dubbed two leading areas of the net on the basis of the leading search queries, compiled monthly by searchterms.com. At the time of writing, the two leading terms have alternated between sex and mp3. Pornography and piracy come together most explicitly in Web areas around the term warez, where in 2000 and 2001 pirated software sites and porn sites have become indistinguishable.

12. See Gerald Wagner, *Körper der Gesellschaft*. Frankfurt/M: Suhrhamp, 1996; and Marc Berg, *Rationalizing Medical Work: Decision Support Techniques and Medical Practices*. Cambridge, MA: MIT Press, 1997.

13. We discuss further knowledge search strategies in Richard Rogers and Andres Zelman, "Surfing for Knowledge in the Information Society," in *Critical Perspectives on the Internet*, ed. Greg Elmer. Lanham, MD: Rowman & Littlefield, 2002: 63–86.

14. See Michael Specter, "Search and Deploy: The Race to Build a Better Search Engine," *New Yorker* (May 29, 2000): 88–100.

15. See Korinna Patelis, "E-Mediation by America Online."

16. See Yaacov Leshem, "Viagra Extends Cuts Vaselife," *Greenhouse Management and Production* 19, no. 10 (October 1999). See also Judy Siegel-Itzkovich, "Viagra makes flowers to stand up straight," *British Medical Journal* 319, no. 7205 (July 1999): 274.

17. Sometimes referred to as a domain name hijacking case, the Leonardo dispute concerned a trademark infringement claim on the Leonardo name made in 1999 by the Transasia Corporation. The most recent ruling has gone in favor of the Leonardo Association, the non-profit arts group which had been using the name for its journal since 1968.

18. See    http://www.pfizer.at/ed/pat/behandlung/Viagra.htm,    accessed    in September 2000.

19. Viagratool.org, accessed in August 2001.

20. "Macht per mail," *De Volkskrant Magazin* (March 24, 2001).

21. http://www.tabloid.net/1998/08/31/Viagra_980831.html, accessed in April 2001.

22. One expert pointed to the consumer success story section at http://www. viagra.com, accessed in April 2001. MR. LESLIE: My name is Robert Leslie. This is my wife Judy. We have been married for 36 years. I have been in a wheelchair for the last 23. When I did get hurt, we lost a lot of stuff, you know, that— I couldn't do anymore. MRS. LESLIE: Going for a walk, holding hands. MR. LESLIE: Yes, it's just different. MRS. LESLIE: A walk on the beach, those are all gone, plus your physical, your sexual life is gone. It's not gone, but it's new, it's a new life that you have to learn to live with. And like he used to come up behind me and put his arm around me and kiss me on my neck, little things that people take for granted.

23. http://www.globalchange.com/Viagranews2.htm, accessed in April 2001.

24. For example, at http://gossipmagazine.com/managearticle.asp?c=80&a=43.

25. http://www.asianfools.com/print.php?sid=92;    and    http://www. animalsagenda.org/articledetail.asp?menu=News&NewsID=188, all accessed in April 2001.

26. http://www.Viagra.com/consumers/about/faq.asp?n=0, accessed in April 2001.

27. *FDA Consumer*, FDA 00–3235 (January–February 2000), http://www. fda.gov/fdac/features/2000/100_online.html, accessed in September 2000.

28. http://www.usrf.org/breakingnews/Viagra_interactions.html, accessed in September 2001.

## Chapter 3

1. The "crisis of democracy" is a reference, among others, to Manuel Castells, *The Power of Identity,* 309–353.

2. On policy exhibitions, see Emilie Gomart and Maarten Hajer, "Is *That* Politics? For an Inquiry into Forms of Contemporary Politics," in *Looking Back, Ahead—The 2002 Yearbook of the Sociology of the Sciences,* eds. Bernward Joerges and Helga Nowotny. Dordrecht: Kluwer, 2003: 33–61.

3. See also Rob Hagendijk, "Public Participation in GM Food; New Methods, Old Politics?" paper presented at the International Conference of the European Association for the Study of Science and Technology (EASST), York, UK, August 31–September 3, 2002; and Rob Hagendijk, "Public Debates as Political Machines," paper presented at the "Concepts of Politics" workshop, organized by the Department of Philosophy, University of Amsterdam, and CSI, Ecole des Mines, Paris, held at Hotel New York, Rotterdam, September 14–15, 2003.

4. See, for example, Linton C. Freeman, "Visualising Social Networks," *Journal of Social Structure* 1, no. 1 (February 2000), http://www2.heinz.cmu.edu/project/INSNA/joss/vsn.html, accessed on February 15, 2003.

5. W. E. Marsden, "The Euro-tunnel as a Case Study: Past and Present," *Teaching Geography* (June 1990): 122–123. The debate table of pros and cons are from E. R. Wethey, "Geography Notes Up-to-date: The Channel Tunnel," *The Practical Teacher* 27 (1906): 397–398.

6. See Jon Turney and Michiel Schwarz, "Holland's great debate on energy," *Town & Country Planning* (March 1983): 79–81. See also Michiel Schwarz and Michael Thompson, *Divided We Stand: Redefining Politics, Technology and Social Choice.* New York: Harvester Wheatsheaf, 1990.

7. The Dutch magazine *Publiek Domain,* by Stichting Weten, continues the tradition of creating Who's Who guides to issues around organized public debates. See, for example, the Who's Who in Xenotransplanation (*Publiek Domein,* July/August, 1998); in the Millennium Bug (*Publiek Domein,* February/March, 1999), and in Climate Change (*Publiek Domein,* April/May, 1999).

8. For the application of the triangulation method, see Richard Rogers and Andrés Zelman, "Surfing for Knowledge in the Information Society."

9. Density is not discussed explicitly here. Whilst our methodological concerns are different, we would share, with Keck and Sikkink, a broadening of the notion of density from traditional network analysis. "Measuring network density is problematic; sufficient densities are likely to be campaign-specific, and not only numbers of 'nodes' in their network but also their quality—access to ability to disseminate information, credibility with targets, ability to speak to and for other social networks—are all important aspects of density as well." Margaret E. Keck and Kathryn Sikkink, *Activists Beyond Borders: Advocacy Networks in International Politics.* Ithaca: Cornell University Press, 1998: 29.

10. Noortje Marres and Richard Rogers, "Depluralising the Web, Repluralising Public Debate: The Case of GM Food on the Web," in *Preferred Placement,* 113–136.

11. On scandal networks, see Noortje Marres, "May the true victim of deface-ment stand up! On reading the network configurations of scandal on the Web," in *Iconoclash: Image-making in Science Religion and Art*, eds. Bruno Latour and Peter Weibel. Cambridge, MA: MIT Press, 2002: 486–489.

12. The piece of research, undertaken with the Information Program at the Open Society Institute in Budapest, has been prospective. The Web issue researchers were to employ the findings for information policy; that is, whether and how to intervene in the issue space around HIV-AIDS in Russia (as well as Belarus and Ukraine). See also the map and information graphics made from the follow-up research in December 2002, entitled "Harm Reduction Networks on the Web: HIV-AIDS in Russia, Ukraine & the Baltics: Comparison between the Russian situation in 2001 & 2002, with connections to select Ukrainian and Baltic networks in 2002," at http://www.govcom.org/publications/drafts/public-health_HIV-AIDS.pdf.

13. United Nations Press Release, DEV/2271 (November 28, 2000).

14. Below is the note (translated by the author) I received from a colleague (Ira van Keulen at Infodrome) that started the food safety debate mapping. "Alge-meen Dagblad and AVRO (www.nederland4.nl) are paying a lot of attention in the next few weeks to the topic of food safety. On their site I came upon quite a few links. Gezondsite.nl has an overview of the issue. Voedsel.net has exten-sive information in its e-zine issues, and some links. Biotechnologie.pagina.nl is a site with hundreds of links to sites about biotechnology. Nrc.nl has a dossier about GM food. Trouw.nl has stuff under health safety and, if you go deeper, you'll come across a dossier on DNA with some old reports as well as the latest news. Pz.nl/akb is the site of the Alternative Consumer Union, where you can read especially about the negative aspects of GM food. Greenpeace.nl has a call to participate in protesting GM crop experiments. Voedselveiligheid.nl is a site with an extensive overview of the issues as well as a clear explanation of what biotechnology is, and also a link list with Dutch and international sites, includ-ing foodnews.org."

15. http://www.pz.nl/akb/Keurmerkenrapport/ToelichtingKM.html, viewed in May 2001.

16. Ministerie van Landbouw, Natuurbeheer en Visserij, en Ministerie van Volksgezondheid, Welzijn en Sport, *Veilig Voedsel in een Veranderende Omgev-ing*, Beleidsnota Voedselveiligheid 2001–2004 (Den Haag, July 2001).

17. Table created on the basis of author's notes.

18. The author has taken part in a series of these events, and has contributed to European Commission projects that rethink the models. Richard Rogers, "Whither Public Participation in Technology?," *EASST Review* 17, no. 4 (December 1998): 40–43; and Richard Rogers, "Spotlight on the European Public Understandings of Science and Technology," *EASST Review* 14, no. 4 (December 1995): 21–23. See also the volumes connected to the events. From the 1995 event, see Meinolf Dierkes and Claudia von Grote, eds. *Between Under-standing and Trust: The Public, Science and Technology*. Amsterdam: Harwood Academic Publishers, 1998. From the 1998 event, see Andrew Jamison and Per

Østby, eds. *Public Participation and Sustainable Development.* Aalborg: Aalborg University Press, 1997; and Andrew Jamison, ed. *Technology Policy Meets the Public.* Aalborg: Aalborg University Press, 1998.

19. For a list of public debate techniques with comparisons, see Wiebe Bijker, *Democratisering van de Technologische Cultuur.* Maastricht: University of Maastricht, 1995; and Wiebe Bijker, "Demokratisierung der Technik—Wer sind die Experten?" in *Aufstand der Laien: Expertentum und Demokratie in der technisierten Welt,* ed. Max Kerner. Aachen: Thouet Verlag, 1997: 133–155.

20. Hivos is the Humanist Institute for Development Co-operation, and may be found at http://www.hivos.nl.

21. The NGOs debate page is http://www.gentechdebat.nl/conferentie, accessed in October 2001.

22. *Financieele Dagblad* (January 10, 2002).

23. *NRC Handelsblad* (January 9, 2002).

24. The government-organized public debate site is http://www.etenengenen.nl, accessed in October 2001.

25. See also Jodi Dean, *Publicity's Secret: How Technoculture Capitalizes on Democracy.* Ithaca, NY: Cornell University Press, 2002.

26. See Alan Irwin and Brian Wynne, "Misunderstood Misunderstandings: Social Identities and the Public Uptake of Science," in *Misunderstanding Science?* eds. Alan Irwin and Brian Wynne. Cambridge, CUP, 1996: 19–46.

27. The early credo read: "Follow the actors." Bruno Latour, *Science in Action: How to Follow Scientists and Engineers Through Society.* Cambridge, MA: Harvard University Press, 1987.

## Chapter 4

1. The making of a third basket—comprising members and partners of the World Economic Forum, mainly multinational corporations which sit at the tables at the annual Davos meeting—was abandoned, for their lack of issues on their Web sites.

2. Helmut Anheier, Marlies Glasius, and Mary Kaldor, eds. *Global Civil Society 2001.* Oxford: OUP, 2001.

3. See http://www.echtewelvaart.nl, accessed July 2001 and through March 2002. While "abstract" in the sense of its name as well as its multi-issue project list, the Echte Welvaart network is also a typically Dutch phenomenon. An initiative of progressive NGOs, it has grown into a Polder model in microcosm, as discussed in chapter 3. At the time of writing it comprises civil society organizations (including faith-based organizations), companies, governmental agencies and ministries, media companies, and universities.

4. Alexander Cockburn, Jeffrey St. Clair, and Allan Sekula, *5 Days that Shook the World: Seattle and Beyond.* London: Verso, 2000.

5. The issue list in itself has become an item of some attention of late. Cf. M. Albright's list of issues for the new president in her Address to Women's Foreign Policy Group in Washington, November 21, 2000 at http://www.usemb.gov.do/IRC/speeches/albrig10.htm: new economy, nonproliferation, environmental issues, women's issues, drugs, HIV-AIDS; and the *New York Times* list directed at the Davos meeting participants (January 30, 2001): environmental damage, water shortages, mass movements of refugees, overpopulation, infectious diseases, Third World poverty.

6. For the Seattle network as agent of social change, see Paul de Armond, "Netwar in the Emerald City: WTO Protest Strategy and Tactics," in *Networks and Netwars: The Future of Terror, Crime and Militancy*, eds. John Arquilla and David Ronfeldt. Santa Monica, CA: RAND, 2001: 201–235.

7. Cf. Dieter Rucht, ed., *Research on Social Movements: The State of the Art in Western Europe and the USA*. Frankfurt/M: Campus, 1991; and Mario Diani, "Social Movements: Virtual and Real," in *Culture and Politics in the Information Age*, ed. Frank Webster. London: Routledge, 2001, 117–128.

8. For a discussion of Oneworld International, see Craig Warkentin, *Reshaping World Politics: NGOs, the Internet and Global Civil Society* (Lanham, MD: Rowman & Littlefield, 2001): 156–168. Note the Indymedia copyright at the bottom of one of its sites: "no(c) Independent Media Center. All content is free for reprint and rebroadcast, on the net and elsewhere, for non-commercial use, unless otherwise noted by author."

9. For some perspective, see the Electronic Frontier Foundation, "Activist Training Manual," presented at the Ruckus Society Tech Toolbox Action Camp, 24 June–2 July, 2002.

10. Cf. *American Behavioural Scientist* 44, no. 10 (June 2001).

11. The e-Development Gateway was renamed the Development Gateway.

12. A flavor of the internal debate on what to call the movement is to be found in the reactions to Katharine Ainger's piece on the history of the anti-global movement, *The Guardian* (23 July 2001). at http://www.indymedia.org/front.php3?article_id=55197, accessed in August 2001.

13. Carlo Giuliani was killed on the streets of Genoa on July 19, 2001.

14. Aileen O'Carroll, "What did you hear about Genoa? Review of TV coverage of the Genoa G8 protests," at http://flag.blackened.net/revolt/wsm/news/2001/genoatv_july.html, accessed in August 2001.

15. Susan George, "The Genoa Protests: Democracy at the barricades," *Le Monde Diplomatique* (August 2001), http://www.en.monde-diplomatique.fr/2001/08/02genoa.

16. To take one example, note the article written by Peter Wood of Boston University, published in the *National Review* (July 25, 2001), http://www.nationalreview.com/comment/comment-wood072501.shtml, and reprinted on Indymedia.org. There are also reactions to his views on the protesters at http://www.indymedia.org/front.php3?article_id=55480&group=webcast.

17. The directions of use for the map are at http://www.genoag8.it/eng/attualita/primo_piano/primo_piano_1.html, accessed in August 2001.

18. Cf. Richard Naylor, Stephan Driver, and James Cornford, "The BBC goes Online: Public Service Broadcasting in the New Media Age," in *Web.Studies*, 137–148.

19. C. Wright Mills, *The Sociological Imagination.* New York: OUP, 1959: 213.

20. Richard Rogers and Noortje Marres, "French Scandals on the Web and on the Streets," 345. See also the concluding chapter of Jodi Dean, *Publicity's Secret.*

21. A brief summary of the major work in this area may be found in Wayne Parsons, *Public Policy.* Cheltenham, UK: Edward Elgar, 1997: 110–120.

22. Cf. Christopher Harper, *And That's the Way It Will Be: News and Information in a Digital World.* New York: New York University Press, 1998; and Diane L. Borden and Kerric Harvey, eds. *The Electronic Grapevine: Rumor, Reputation, and Reporting in the New On-Line Environment.* Mahwah, NJ: Lawrence Erlbaum Associates, 1998.

23. Naomi Klein, "Reclaiming the Commons," *New Left Review* 9 (May/June 2001): 81–89.

24. Susanna Hornig Priest, *A Grain of Truth: The Media, the Public and Biotechnology.* Lanham, MD: Rowman & Littlefield, 2001: 120.

25. Bernardo Huberman, *Laws of the Web.*

26. See Amy Harmon's piece entitled "Exploration of World Wide Web Tilts From Eclectic to Mundane," in the *New York Times* (August 26, 2001).

27. I discuss the "hit economy" in Richard Rogers, "Operating Issue Networks on the Web," *Science as Culture* 11, no. 2 (2002): 191–213.

28. "How did stock tickers become more ubiquitous on television than weather forecasts?" For the rise of the "ticker mentality," see Thomas Frank, *One Market Under God: Extreme Capitalism, Market Populism and the End of Economic Democracy.* New York: Doubleday, 2000.

29. John Keane, *Civil Society: Old Images, New Visions.* Palo Alto, CA: Stanford UP, 1999.

30. This example is taken directly from Greenpeace's framing of climate change as issue on http://www.greenpeace.org, accessed in August 2001.

31. Lev Manovich, "The Poetics of Augmented Reality: Learning from Prada," unpublished ms. (February 2002), http://www.manovich.net/DOCS/augmented_space.doc.

32. http://50.lycos.com.

33. http://www.google.com/press/zeitgeist.html.

## Chapter 5

1. Cf. Anthony Downs, "Up and Down with Ecology," *The Public Interest* 28 (Summer 1972): 38–50.

2. The Labour Party (PvdA), the majority party of the ruling Purple Coalition, was first to publish its election platform on September 1, 2001 at http://www.pvda.nl/hot/vkp2002/vkp_intro.htm. The Socialist Party's (SP) followed shortly after at http://www.sp.nl/partij/theorie/program.

3. See also Geoffrey C. Bowker and Susan Leigh Star, *Sorting Things Out: Classification and its Consequences.* Cambridge, MA: MIT Press, 1999.

4. As of January 2003 *De Telegraaf* archive is at http://wwwijzer.nl/ NieuwsArchief, *de Volkskrant* at http://zoek.volkskrant.nl, and the *NRC Handelsblad* at http://archief.nrc.nl. For each archive, note that searches are performed for the print versions.

5. Nicholas Baker, *Double Fold Libraries and the Assault on Paper.* New York: Random House, 2001.

6. Based on the work of James Heckman and others, "propensity weighting" in telephone polling allows the poller to take into account the views of those people who do *not* answer the telephone.

7. The advent of Rich Site Summary (RSS) streams, and also the readers that allow selected sets of press sources (channels) to be fed to the desktop, is now a promising avenue to undertake such a divining exercise. For TV news capturing and analysis, see also the Open Directory Project's list of media monitors at http://dmoz.org/News/Services/Media_Monitoring.

8. For all issue attention graphs undertaken for the Labour Party campaign platform and the Echte Welvaart multi-issue movement, July–October 2001, see http://www.govcom.org/non_issue.

9. "Medien hielp populisme" is how a Dutch political weekly summarised the research. *P.M. Den Haag* 43 (November 2002): 1.

10. See de Volkskrant, *Het fenomeen Fortuyn.* Amsterdam: Meulenhoff, 2002: 113–115; and Dick Pels, *De Geest van Pim.* Amsterdam: Anthos, 2003. See also Pim Fortuyn, *De Puinhopen van Acht Jaar Paars.* Rotterdam: Karakter Uitgevers, 2002.

11. The Dutch political scientist Philip van Praag published an article the day before the elections predicting, with reference to its media attention, the rise of another "protest party"—the Animals' Party (Partij voor de Dieren). Philip van Praag, "Reële kans voor politieke dieren," http://www.politiek-digitaal.nl/ nieuwedemocratie/kans_voor_politiekedieren.shtml, posted on January 21, 2003. The party failed to win a seat.

12. http://www.politiek-digitaal.nl. Note the Election Issue Tracker is not currently measuring the press resonance of non-issues.

13. Cf. Dorothy Nelkin, *Selling Science: How the Press covers Science and Technology.* New York: W.H. Freeman, 1988.

14. For the NGO variety, see http://www.greenmediatoolshed.org.

15. Manuel Castells, *The Power of Identity*, 343.

16. Cf. Justin Lewis, Michael Morgan, and Andy Ruddock, "Images/Issues/ Impact: The Media And Campaign '92," A Report by the Center for the Study

of Communication, University of Massachusetts at Amherst, 1992, http://www.umass.edu/communication/resources/special_reports/campaign_92/index.shtml.

17. The four parties that did not change their platforms are the Socialist Party (SP), the Political Reform Party (SGP), the Christian Union (ChristenUnie), and the Liberal Party (VVD). Three parties changed their slogans. Green Left (Groen Links): Overvloed en Onbehagen (2002), Protest en Perspectief (2003); Labour (PvdA): Samen voor de Toekomst (2002), Voor Solidariteit, Verantwoordelijkheid en Respect (2003); and Liveable Netherlands (Leefbaar Nederland): no slogan (2002), Deze keer doen ze echt wat ze beloven. Toch? (2003).

## Chapter 6

1. We are doing situated information politics, and thereby not substituting information for reality, an issue critically raised in Albert Borgmann, *Holding on to Reality*. Chicago: University of Chicago Press, 1999.

2. We thereby depart from the classic definition of information politics as being about collecting and reporting facts and packaging them in ways to make them suitable for press consumption or the court of law. Cf. Margaret Keck and Kathryn Sikkink, *Activists Beyond Borders*, 18–22.

3. Stephan Coleman, "Strong Representation," unpublished ms. (2000).

4. Cf. Stephen Coleman and John Gotze, eds. *Bowling Together: Online Public Engagement in Policy Deliberation*. London: Hansard, 2001; and Steven Clift, "Online Consultations and Events: Top Ten Tips for Government and Civic Hosts," 2002, http://www.publicus.net/articles/consult.html, accessed on April 15, 2002.

5. Lawrence Lessig, *Code and other Laws of Cyberspace: How Will the Architecture of Cyberspace Change the Constitution?* New York: Basic Books, 1999.

6. Here it may be remarked that *FirstMonday*, a leading online-only journal of Internet study, has failed repeatedly in their efforts to be taken up by the Science Citation Index. Personal conversation with the editor, November 5, 2001. The suggestion was made to add page numbers.

7. Howard Rheingold, ed., *The Millennium Whole Earth Catalog*. San Francisco: HarperCollins, 1994: 263.

8. Cf. Annelise Riles, *The Network Inside Out*. Ann Arbor: University of Michigan Press, 2001: 23–69; John Arquilla and David Ronfeldt, *Networks and Netwars*; John Naughton, "Contested Space: The Internet and Global Civil Society," *Global Civil Society 2001*, 147–168; and Craig Warkentin, *Reshaping World Politics*.

# Bibliography

Aikens, G. Scott. "A History of Minnesota Electronic Democracy 1994," *FirstMonday* 1, no. 5 (November 1996), http://www.firstmonday.dk/issues/issue5/aikens.

*American Behavioural Scientist* 44, no. 10 (June 2001).

American Civil Liberties Union. *Censorship in a Box: Why Blocking Software Is Wrong for Public Libraries*. Wye Mills, MD: ACLU, 1998.

American Civil Liberties Union. *Fahrenheit 451.2: Is Cyberspace Burning? How Rating and Blocking Proposals May Torch Free Speech on the Internet*. Wye Mills, MD: ACLU, 1997.

Anheier, Helmut, Marlies Glasius, and Mary Kaldor, eds. *Global Civil Society 2001*. Oxford: OUP, 2001.

Armond, Paul de. "Netwar in the Emerald City: WTO Protest Strategy and Tactics," in *Networks and Netwars: The Future of Terror, Crime and Militancy*, ed. John Arquilla and David Ronfeldt. Santa Monica, CA: RAND, 2001: 201–235.

Arnett, Nick. "Mendicant Sysops in Cyberspace," *TidBITS* 225/09 (May 1994), http://www.tidbits.com/tb-issues/TidBITS-225.html.

Arquilla, John and David Ronfeldt, eds. *Networks and Netwars: The Future of Terror, Crime and Militancy*. Santa Monica, CA: RAND, 2001.

Athanasekou, P. E. "Internet and Copyright: An Introduction to Caching, Linking and Framing," *The Journal of Information, Law and Technology* 2 (1998), http://elj.warwick.ac.uk/jilt/wip/98_2atha.

Baker, Nicholas. *Double Fold Libraries and the Assault on Paper*. New York: Random House, 2001.

Barabási, Alberto-László. *Linked: The New Science of Networks*. Cambridge, MA: Perseus, 2002.

Barber, Benjamin R. "Three Scenarios for the Future of Technology and Strong Democracy," *Political Science Quarterly* 113, no. 4 (1999): 573–589.

Barbrook, Richard and Andy Cameron. "The Californian Ideology," *Science as Culture* 6, no. 26 (1996): 44–72.

Beck, Ulrich. *Risikogesellschaft: Auf dem Weg in eine andere Moderne.* Frankfurt/M: Suhrkamp Verlag, 1986.

Berg, Marc. *Rationalizing Medical Work: Decision Support Techniques and Medical Practices.* Cambridge, MA: MIT Press, 1997.

Berners-Lee, Tim and Mark Fishcetti. *Weaving the Web: The Original Design and Ultimate Destiny of the World Wide Web by its Inventor.* San Francisco: HarperCollins, 1999.

Bijker, Wiebe. "Demokratisierung der Technik: Wer sind die Experten?" in *Aufstand der Laien: Expertentum und Demokratie in der technisierten Welt,* ed. Max Kerner. Aachen: Thouet Verlag, 1997: 133–155.

Bijker, Wiebe. *Democratisering van de Technologische Cultuur.* Maastricht: University of Maastricht, 1995.

Bolter, Jay David and Richard Grusin. *Remediation: Understanding New Media.* Cambridge, MA: MIT Press, 2000.

Borden, Diane L. and Kerric Harvey, eds. *The Electronic Grapevine: Rumor, Reputation and Reporting in the New On-Line Environment.* Mahwah, NJ: Lawrence Erlbaum Associates, 1998.

Borgmann, Albert. *Holding on to Reality.* Chicago: University of Chicago Press, 1999.

Bowker, Geoffrey C. and Susan Leigh Star. *Sorting Things Out: Classification and its Consequences.* Cambridge, MA: MIT Press, 1999.

Branscomb, Anne. *Who Owns Information? From Privacy to Public Access.* New York: Basic Books, 1995.

Bush, Vannevar. "As We May Think," *Atlantic Monthly* 176, no. 1 (July 1945): 101–108.

Calishain, Tara and Rael Dornfest. *Google Hacks.* San Sebastopol, CA: O'Reilly, 2003.

Callon, Michiel, John Law, and Arie Rip, eds. *Mapping the Dynamics of Science & Society.* London: Macmillan Press, 1986.

Castells, Manuel. *The Power of Identity.* Oxford: Blackwell, 1997.

Chalmers, Matthew. "Cookies Are Not Enough: Tracking and Enriching Web Activity with a Recommender System," in *Preferred Placement: Knowledge Politics on the Web,* ed. Richard Rogers. Maastricht: Jan van Eyck Editions, 2000: 99–111.

Clift, Steven. "Online Consultations and Events: Top Ten Tips for Government and Civic Hosts," (2002), http://www.publicus.net/articles/consult.html.

Cockburn, Alexander, Jeffrey St. Clair, and Allan Sekula. *5 Days that Shook the World: Seattle and Beyond.* London: Verso, 2000.

Coleman, Stephan. "Strong Representation," unpublished ms. (2000).

Coleman, Stephen and John Gotze, eds. *Bowling Together: Online Public Engagement in Policy Deliberation.* London: Hansard, 2001.

Dean, Jodi. *Publicity's Secret: How Technoculture Capitalizes on Democracy.* Ithaca, NY: Cornell University Press, 2002.

Dean, Jodi. "Virtual Fears," *Signs: Journal of Women in Culture and Society* 24, no. 4 (1999): 1069–1078.

Dean, Jodi. "Virtually Citizens," *Constellations* 4, no. 2 (1997): 264–281.

Diani, Mario. "Social Movements: Virtual and Real," in *Culture and Politics in the Information Age*, ed. Frank Webster. London: Routledge, 2001: 117–128.

Dierkes, Meinolf and Claudia von Grote, eds. *Between Understanding and Trust: The Public, Science and Technology.* Amsterdam: Harwood Academic Publishers, 1998.

Downs, Anthony. "Up and Down with Ecology," *The Public Interest* 28 (Summer 1972): 38–50.

Dreyfus, Herbert. *On the Internet.* London: Routledge, 2001.

Dunne, Anthony. *Hertzian Tales.* London: Royal College of Art, 2000.

Electronic Frontier Foundation. "Activist Training Manual," presented at the Ruckus Society Tech Toolbox Action Camp, June 24–July 2, 2002.

*FDA Consumer.* FDA 00-3235 (January–February, 2000).

Elmer, Greg. *Profiling Machines: Mapping the Personal Information Economy.* Cambridge, MA: MIT Press, 2004.

Elmer, Greg. "Hypertext on the Web: The Beginning and End of Web Path-ology," *Space and Culture* 10 (2001): 1–14.

Fishkin, James. *The Voice of the People: Public Opinion and Democracy.* New Haven: Yale University Press, 1997.

Fishkin, James. *Democracy and Deliberation: New Directions for Democratic Reform.* New Haven: Yale University Press, 1991.

Fortier, François. *Virtuality Check.* London: Verso, 2001.

Fortuyn, Pim. *De Puinhopen van Acht Jaar Paars.* Rotterdam: Karakter Uitgevers, 2002.

Fox, Edward. *The Hungarian who Walked to Heaven: Alexander Csoma de Körös, 1784–1842.* London: Short Books, 2001.

Frank, Thomas. *One Market Under God: Extreme Capitalism. Market Populism and the End of Economic Democracy.* New York: Doubleday, 2000.

Freeman, Linton C. "Visualising Social Networks," *Journal of Social Structure* 1, no. 1 (February 2000), http://www2.heinz.cmu.edu/project/INSNA/joss/vsn.html.

Gandy, Oscar. *The Panoptic Sort: A Political Economy of Personal Information.* Boulder, CO: Westview Press, 1993.

George, Susan. "The Genoa Protests: Democracy at the Barricades," *Le Monde Diplomatique* (August 2001), http://www.en.monde-diplomatique.fr/2001/08/02genoa.

Gomart, Emilie and Maarten Hajer. "Is *That* Politics? For an Inquiry into Forms of Contemporary Politics," in *Looking Back, Ahead: The 2002 Yearbook of the Sociology of the Sciences*, ed. Bernward Joerges and Helga Nowotny. Dordrecht: Kluwer, 2003: 33–61.

Grusin, Richard. "Pre-mediation," *Criticism* (forthcoming).

Gurstein, Michael, ed. *Community Informatics: Enabling Communities with Information and Communications Technologies*. Hershey, PA: Idea Group, 2000.

Hagendijk, Rob. "Public Debates as Political Machines," paper presented at the "Concepts of Politics" workshop organized by the Department of Philosophy, University of Amsterdam, and Ecole des Mines, Paris, held at Hotel New York, Rotterdam, September, 14–15 2003.

Hagendijk, Rob. "Public participation in GM Food; New Methods, Old Politics?" paper presented at the International Conference of the European Association for the Study of Science and Technology (EASST), York, UK, August 31–September 3, 2002.

Hague, Barry and Brian Loader, eds. *Digital Democracy: Discourse and Decision Making in the Information Age*. London: Routledge, 1999.

Harper, Christopher. *And That's the Way It Will Be: News and Information in a Digital World*. New York: New York University Press, 1998.

Hill, Kevin and John E. Hughes, eds. *Cyberpolitics: Citizen Activism in the Age of the Internet*. Lanham, MD: Rowman & Littlefield, 1998.

Huberman, Bernardo. *The Laws of the Web*. Cambridge, MA: MIT Press, 2001.

Introna, Lucas and Helen Nissenbaum (2000). "Shaping the Web: Why the Politics of Search Engines Matter," *The Information Society* 16, no. 3: 169–186.

Introna, Lucas and Helen Nissenbaum. "The Public Good Vision of the Internet and the Politics of Search Engines," in *Preferred Placement: Knowledge Politics on the Web*, ed. Richard Rogers. Maastricht: Jan van Eyck Editions, 2000: 25–47.

Jones, Steve, ed. *Encyclopedia of New Media*. Thousand Oaks. CA: Sage, 2003.

Jones, Steve, ed. *Doing Internet Research: Critical Issues and Methods for Examining the Net*. London: Sage, 1999.

Keane, John. *Civil Society: Old Images, New Visions*. Palo Alto, CA: Stanford UP, 1999.

Keeble, Leigh and Brian Loader, eds. *Community Informatics: Shaping Computer-Mediated Social Networks*. London: Routledge, 2001.

Klein, Naomi. "Reclaiming the Commons," *New Left Review* 9 (May/June 2001): 81–89.

Kling, Rob, Joanna Fortuna, and Adam King. "The Real Stakes of Virtual Publishing: The Transformation of E-Biomed into PubMed Central," CIS working paper WP-01-03, SLIS, Indiana University, 2001, http://www.slis.indiana.edu/CSI/WP/kling3.pdf.

Kraus, Karl. *Die letzten Tage der Menschheit*. Frankfurt/M: Suhrkamp Verlag, 1992.

Irwin, Alan and Brian Wynne. "Misunderstood Misunderstandings: Social Identities and the Public Uptake of Science," in *Misunderstanding Science?* eds. Alan Irwin and Brian Wynne. Cambridge, CUP, 1996: 19–46.

Jamison, Andrew, ed. *Technology Policy Meets the Public.* Aalborg: Aalborg University Press, 1998.

Jamison, Andrew and Per Østby, eds. *Public Participation and Sustainable Development.* Aalborg: Aalborg University Press, 1997.

Keck, Margaret E. and Kathryn Sikkink. *Activists beyond Borders: Advocacy Networks in International Politics.* Ithaca, NY: Cornell University Press, 1998.

Körös, Alexander Csoma de. *Grammar of the Tibetan Language.* Budapest: Akademiai Kiado, 1984.

Körös, Alexander Csoma de. *Tibetan Studies.* Budapest: Akademiai Kiado, 1984.

Körös, Alexander Csoma de. *A Dictionary of Tibetan and English.* New Delhi: Cosmo, 1978.

Langer, James. "Physicists in the New Era of Electronic Publishing," *Physics Today Online* 53, no. 8 (August 2000): 35, http://www.aip.org/pt/vol-53/iss-8/p35.html.

Latour, Bruno. *We Have Never Been Modern,* trans. Catherine Porter. New York: Harvester Wheatsheaf, 1993.

Latour, Bruno. *Science in Action: How to Follow Scientists and Engineers Through Society.* Cambridge, MA: Harvard University Press, 1987.

Lawrence, Steve and C. Lee Giles. "Accessibility of Information on the Web," *Nature* 400 (1999): 107–109.

Lawrence, Steve and C. Lee Giles. "Searching the Web," *Science* 280 (1998): 98–100.

Leshem, Yaacov. "Viagra Extends Cuts Vaselife," *Greenhouse Management and Production* 19, no. 10 (October 1999).

Lessig, Lawrence. *Code and other Laws of Cyberspace.* New York: Basic Books, 1999.

Lewis, Justin, Michael Morgan, and Andy Ruddock. "Images/Issues/Impact: The Media And Campaign '92," A report by the Center for the Study of Communication, University of Massachusetts at Amherst, 1992, http://www.umass.edu/communication/resources/special_reports/campaign_92/index.shtml.

Lippmann, Walter. *Public Opinion.* New York: Free Press, 1997.

Ludlow, Peter, ed. *Cryto Anarchy, Cyberstates and Pirate Utopias.* Cambridge, MA: MIT Press, 2001.

Manovich, Lev. "The Poetics of Augmented Reality: Learning from Prada," unpublished ms. (February 2002).

Manovich, Lev. *The Language of New Media.* Cambridge, MA: MIT Press, 2001.

Marres, Noortje. "May the True Victim of Defacement Stand Up! On Reading the Network Configurations of Scandal on the Web." in *Iconoclash. Image-making in Science Religion and Art*, eds. Bruno Latour and Peter Weibel. Cambridge, MA: MIT Press, 2002: 486–489.

Marres, Noortje. "Somewhere you've got to draw the line: De politiek van selectie op het Web." M.Sc. thesis, University of Amsterdam, 2000.

Marres, Noorjte and Gerard de Vries. *Tussen toegang en kwaliteit: legitimatie en contestatie van expertise op het Internet*, Voorstudie, Wetenschappelijke Raad voor het Regeringsbeleid, Den Haag, 2002.

Marres, Noortje and Richard Rogers. "Depluralising the Web, Repluralising Public Debate: The Case of GM Food on the Web," in *Preferred Placement: Knowledge Politics on the Web*, ed. Richard Rogers. Maastricht: Jan van Eyck Editions, 2000: 113–136.

Marsden, W. E. "The Euro-tunnel as a Case Study: past and present," *Teaching Geography* (June 1990): 122–123.

Miller, Vincent. "Search Engines, Portals and Global Capitalism," in *Web.Studies*, ed. David Gauntlett. London: Arnold, 2000: 113–121.

Mills, C. Wright. *The Sociological Imagination*. New York: OUP, 1959.

Ministerie van Landbouw, Natuurbeheer en Visserij, and Ministerie van Volksgezondheid, Welzijn en Sport. *Veilig voedsel in een veranderende omgeving*, Beleidsnota voedselveiligheid 2001–2004, Den Haag, July 18, 2001.

Moglen, Eben. "Anarchism Triumphant: Free Software and the Death of Copyright," *FirstMonday* 4, no. 8 (1999), http://www.firstmonday.org/issues/issue4_8/moglen.

Naylor, Richard, Stephan Driver, and James Cornford. "The BBC goes Online: Public Service Broadcasting in the New Media Age," in *Web.Studies*, ed. David Gauntlett. London: Arnold, 2000: 137–148.

Negroponte, Nicholas. *Being Digital*. New York: Alfred A. Knopf, 1995.

Nyce, James and Paul Kahn, eds. *From Memex to Hypertext: Vannevar Bush and the Mind's Machine*. New York: Academic Press, 1991.

Parsons, Wayne. *Public Policy*. Cheltenham, UK: Edward Elgar, 1997.

Patelis, Korinna. "E-mediation by America Online," in *Preferred Placement: Knowledge Politics on the Web*, ed. Richard Rogers. Maastricht: Jan van Eyck Editions, 2000: 49–63.

Pels, Dick. *De Geest van Pim*. Amsterdam: Anthos, 2003.

Poster, Mark. "Cyberdemocracy: Internet and the Public Sphere," in *Internet Culture*, ed. David Porter. New York: Routledge, 1997: 201–218.

Priest, Susanna Hornig. *A Grain of Truth: The Media, the Public and Biotechnology*. Lanham, MD: Rowman & Littlefield, 2001.

Resnick, Paul and Hal Varian. "Recommender Systems," *Communications of the ACM* 40, no. 3 (1997): 56, 58.

Princeton Survey Research Associates. "A Matter of Trust: What Users Want from Websites. Results of a National Survey of Internet Researchers for Consumer WebWatch," January 2002.

Praag, Philip van. "Reële kans voor politieke dieren," politiek-digitaal.nl (January 21, 2003), http://www.politiek-digitaal.nl/nieuwedemocratie/kans_voor_politiekedieren.shtml.

*P. M. Den Haag.* 43 (November 2002): 1.

*Publiek Domein* (July/August 1998).

*Publiek Domein* (February/March 1999).

*Publiek Domein* (April/May 1999).

Rheingold, Howard. *Smart Mobs.* Cambridge, MA: Perseus, 2003.

Rheingold, Howard, ed. *The Millennium Whole Earth Catalog.* San Francisco: HarperCollins, 1994.

Riles, Annelise. *The Network Inside Out.* Ann Arbor: University of Michigan Press, 2001.

Rogers, Richard. "Operating Issue Networks on the Web," *Science as Culture* 11, no. 2 (2002): 191–213.

Rogers, Richard. "Introduction: Towards the Practice of Web Epistemology," in *Preferred Placement: Knowledge Politics on the Web,* ed. Richard Rogers. Maastricht: Jan van Eyck Editions, 2000: 11–23.

Rogers, Richard. "Whither Public Participation in Technology?" *EASST Review* 17, no. 4 (December 1998): 40–43.

Rogers, Richard. "Spotlight on the European Public Understandings of Science and Technology," *EASST Review* 14, no. 4 (December 1995): 21–23.

Rogers, Richard and Noortje Marres. "French Scandals on the Web and on the Streets: A Small Experiment in Stretching the Limits of Reported Reality," *Asian Journal of Social Science* 30, no. 2 (2002): 339–353.

Rogers, Richard and Andrés Zelman. "Surfing for Knowledge in the Information Society," in *Critical Perspectives on the Internet,* ed. Greg Elmer. Lanham, MD: Rowman & Littlefield, 2002: 63–86.

Ronfeldt, David and John Arquilla. "Networks, Netwars and the Fight for the Future," *FirstMonday* 6, no. 10 (2001), http://www.firstmonday.dk/issues/issue6_10/ronfeldt.

Rucht, Dieter, ed. *Research on Social Movements: The State of the Art in Western Europe and the USA.* Frankfurt/M: Campus, 1991.

Schwarz, Michiel and Michael Thompson. *Divided We Stand: Redefining Politics, Technology and Social Choice.* New York: Harvester Wheatsheaf, 1990.

Shapiro, Andrew. "Street Corners in Cyberspace," *The Nation* (July 3, 1995): 10–14.

Shaw, Debora. "Playing the Links: Interactivity and Stickiness in .Com and 'Not.Com' Web Sites," *FirstMonday* 6, no. 3 (2001), http://www.firstmonday.dk/issues/issue6_3/shaw.

Siegel-Itzkovich, Judy. "Viagra makes flowers stand up straight," *British Medical Journal* 319, no. 7205 (July 31, 1999): 274.

Slevin, James. *Internet and Society*. London: Polity Press, 2000.

Specter, Michael. "Search and Deploy: The Race to Build a Better Search Engine," *New Yorker* (May 29, 2000): 88–100.

Stuurgroep Maatschappelijke Discussie Energiebeleid. *Eindrapport van de Brede Maatschappelijke Discussie Energiebeleid*. Den Haag: Stenfert Kroese, 1983.

Sunstein, Cass. *Republic.com*. Princeton. NJ: Princeton University Press, 2001.

Tann, Jennifer, Adrian Platts, Sarah Welch, and Judy Allen. "Patient Power? Medical Perspectives on the Patient Use of the Internet," *Prometheus* 21, no. 2 (2003): 145–160.

Tsagarousianou, Roza, Damian Tambini, and Cathy Bryan, eds. *Cyberdemocracy: Technology, Cities and Civic Networks*. London: Routledge, 1998.

Turney, Jon and Michiel Schwarz. "Holland's Great Debate on Energy," *Town & Country Planning* (March 1983): 79–81.

United Nations Press Release. DEV/2271 (November 28, 2000).

De Volkskrant. *Het fenomeen Fortuyn*. Amsterdam: Meulenhoff, 2000.

Wagner, Gerald. *Körper der Gesellschaft*. Frankfurt/M.: Suhrkamp, 1996.

Wakeford, Nina. "New Media, New Methodologies: Studying the Web," in *Web.Studies*, ed. David Gauntlett. London: Arnold, 2000: 31–41.

Warkentin, Craig. *Reshaping World Politics: NGOs, the Internet and Global Civil Society*. Lanham, MD: Rowman & Littlefield, 2000.

Warner, Michael. *Publics and Counterpublics*. New York: Zone Books, 2002.

Wesemael, Pieter van. *Architecture of Instruction and Delight: A Socio-Historical Analysis of the World Exhibition as a Didactic Phenomenon, 1798–1851–1970*. Rotterdam: 010, 2001.

Wethey, E. R. "Geography Notes Up-to-date: The Channel Tunnel," *The Practical Teacher* 27 (1906): 397–398.

Wilhelm, Anthony G. "Virtual Sounding Boards: How Deliberative Is Online Political Discussion?" in *Digital Democracy: Discourse and Decision Making in the Information Age*, eds. Barry N. Hague and Brian D. Loader. London: Routledge, 1999: 154–178.

Woolgar, Steve. "Configuring the User: The Case of Usability Trials," in *A Sociology of Monsters: Essays on Power, Technology and Domination*. ed. John Law. London: Routledge, 1991: 57–99.

# Index